BUILDING GODLY HABITS:

A SPIRITUAL BUILDING PLAN
8 HABITS FOR GODLY LIVING

Sheri,
May God's grace abound
in your life.
Sincerely,
Pastor Earnestine Blakley
10-5-19

BUILDING GODLY HABITS

A Spiritual Building Plan

8 Habits for Godly Living

PASTOR EARNESTINE BLAKLEY

PORTLAND • OREGON
INKWATERPRESS.COM

Scan QR Code to learn more about this title

Cover and interior design by Jayme Vincent

Christian Cross © PalokhaTetiana. BigStockPhoto.com

Publisher: Inkwater Press | www.inkwaterpress.com

Paperback
ISBN-13 978-1-62901-193-6 | ISBN-10 1-62901-193-2

Printed in the U.S.A.
All paper is acid free and meets all ANSI standards for archival quality paper.

1 3 5 7 9 10 8 6 4 2

DEDICATION

This book is dedicated first and foremost to God, who gave me the desire and motivation to write this book; to my beloved husband, Charles Sr., and to our adult sons, Charles Jr. and Andrew Blakley, who support me and encourage me in all of my endeavors; to my deceased father, Thomas Bob Ross, and my living mother, Mary Anna Ross, who encouraged me as a child to always follow my dreams and to always put God first; to my deceased father-in-law and mother-in-law, David and Lula Blakley, who were role models of hard work and the value of getting an education; to my brothers, sisters, sisters-in-law, brothers-in-law, relatives, and loved ones who sharpened me with words of wisdom and guidance; to the members and friends of Hope Fellowship Church and H.O.P.E. Outreach Ministries, Inc. who keep me lifted up in prayer and who help me accomplish the purpose that God has ordained for me; and to everyone in my sphere of influence who has helped me do God's work. My life is a composite of many people who have come alongside to help me advance the Kingdom of God in spreading the Gospel of Jesus Christ. To everyone, I say "Thank You!"

CONTENTS

INTRODUCTION

At the beginning of every year, it is customary to establish "New Year's Resolutions." Nevertheless, these resolutions are easier said than done. Have you ever wondered why in the midst of your good intentions, you still failed to maintain the most well-meaning resolutions? The answer to this dilemma is habit. We are creatures of habit; therefore, it is necessary to have a paradigm shift. We need to consciously develop spiritual habits by repetitiously doing Godly things—Godly means behavior that is consistent with the nature of God. If we want to implement our spiritual resolutions, we must develop a pattern of behavior that will be conducive to developing that desired behavioral change.

Have you ever wondered how habits are formed? Habits are formed strategically and methodically. A habit is a pattern of behavior that is acquired through repetition. Experts say that it takes twenty-one days to make a habit. Habits are built one day at a time. Building each Godly habit requires consistency in doing Godly things. Can you imagine the magnitude of our spiritual growth if we were to develop the eight habits mentioned in this book? Each habit is built day by day, week by week, and month by month. With the help of the Holy Spirit, we can be built into healthier Christians.

God's word says in Psalm 127:1 (NIV): *Unless the LORD builds the house, its builders labor in vain.*

God is our architect. We must allow Him to design us one brick at a time. Each habit becomes a pattern in God's omnipotent masterpiece. It takes much practice to be conformed into the image of our Lord and Savior, Jesus Christ. The word "build" means to make by combining parts or to add gradually. This means that we are a work in progress. We do not become a complete spiritual house overnight. The same is true with any physical exercise. If we are striving to lose weight, we don't lose a massive amount overnight. It takes time. For this reason, many people have a "before" and "after" picture of themselves when setting a weight-loss goal. I would challenge you to have a before and after spiritual picture of yourself by writing down your spiritual goals. Therefore, at the end of at least eight months, you will be able to assess your spiritual progress. It is a good idea to ask those who are close to you to critique your spiritual image. Just remember that God is not finished with us. We will continue to be a work in progress until we reach our heavenly home.

Building Godly habits must be deliberate and intentional. When we are truly serious about becoming more like Jesus, we will make strides to build ourselves in that direction. For example if we want to rise at 6:00 a.m. each morning, we will set an alarm clock for that time. After many mornings of our alarm clock sounding off at 6:00 a.m., it becomes a habit to rise at that time. As a matter of fact, it becomes internalized. We will wake up right at 6:00 a.m. even if the alarm clock is not activated. Why? We are creatures of habit. The pattern of repetition comes into reality.

The same is true with our spiritual lives. If we deliberately devise a plan to build a specific habit, we will accomplish that behavior after at least twenty-one days. By being repetitious, we will find ourselves exercising Godly habits without even thinking about it. Nevertheless, sacrifices will have to be made. We must be willing to give up one thing in order to gain another. We cannot keep exhibiting the same bad habits and expect to get new results. We must do what we have never done before in order to achieve what we have never achieved.

This book addresses eight habits for Godly living. Eight is the number for new beginnings. Let's begin our building exercise together—building our spiritual houses one brick at a time! Each month we will focus on developing a new habit. After about eight months, since it takes about twenty-one days to make a habit, we will be more conformed into the image of Jesus Christ. How exciting!

CHAPTER ONE

THE HABIT OF VISION

Where there is no vision, the people perish.

Proverbs 29:18 (KJV)

STAY FOCUSED

Have you ever been driving down the road and a deer or some animal crossed your path, causing you to swerve in order to miss the forlorn creature? Well, that swerving motion can actually cause you to land in the ditch or have a serious wreck. In a spiritual sense, whenever we are traveling along God's path and become distracted, we can literally become so distracted that we land totally off of the path that God has intended for us.

There are many "swerving" Christians in the world. The key is to stay focused—finding a fixed point of concentration. In order to become like Jesus, we must formulate a vision and stay focused on that vision. We magnify whatever we focus on at a particular moment. Focusing on Jesus causes us to magnify Him!

God's word says in Hebrews 12:2a (NIV): *Let us fix our eyes on Jesus, the author and perfecter of our faith.*

Jesus is such a solidified point that we are guaranteed a straight path. Our focus must be on Him despite the trials we encounter, and by the way, the trials will come! Whatever shakes us up should not shake us off the path that God has designed for us. We need to pray and ask God to give us a vision that we can stay focused on until we reach that particular spiritual goal. According to *Webster's New Compact Dictionary*, a vision is seeing ahead or having foresight. We must begin to see ourselves as becoming the person that God wants us to become. In order to do this, we must begin with the end in mind.

When I was growing up, I was raised on a farm, the second oldest of fourteen children. My parents grew soybean, cotton, and wheat. With those staple crops to manage, my older siblings and I worked approximately ten hours a day. As the blazing hot sun beamed down on the side of my face, I would dream of getting an education and becoming a school teacher. Having that dream in front of me made the long summer hours more tolerable. I knew that getting an education would be a path that would get me out of this type of livelihood. I learned to begin each day with the end in mind. Not one day passed that I didn't dream of becoming a school teacher. I even practiced teaching by teaching my younger brothers and sisters the alphabet, their multiplication facts, and other educational requirements. Every day I knew the time would come when I would no longer have to work in the open sun and elements all day in order to make a living. Of course, whenever it rained, those were opportunities for a long-awaited break.

Proverbs 29:18a (KJV) says: *Where there is no vision, the people perish.*

I am a witness that without a vision or focus, dreams are unattainable. If we aim at nothing, we will hit it every time. Every target can be a bull's eye when Jesus is guiding the arrow. Jesus must be the arm that launches us forward. Jesus charted my course to become an elementary school teacher; He later directed me to start an outreach ministry that reaches hundreds of people a year. A few years later, He called me to be a Pastor whereby I reach hundreds of people through the church and the TV and radio ministry.

Staying focused has enabled me to accomplish numerous opportunities that would have been impossible without a vision.

WAYS TO STAY FOCUSED

One way to stay focused on the vision is to "Write the Vision."

Habakkuk 2:2–3 (NKJV) says: *Write the vision and make it plain on tablets, that he may run who reads it. For the vision is yet for an appointed time; but at the end it will speak, and it will not lie. Though it tarries, wait for it; because it will surely come, it will not tarry.*

When the vision is written, we are able to keep it before us. We must be certain that it is in a visible place so that we can read it every day. Reading the vision out aloud implants it in our mind and soul. It literally becomes a part of us.

Writing the vision helps us to acquire a revelation of who Jesus is and what He can do for us. We must have an epiphany whereby we get a revelation of Jesus Christ as He manifests Himself to us personally. We must have our own individual testimony of who Jesus is to us. The prophet Isaiah summed it up beautifully when he said: *"I saw the*

Lord sitting on a throne, high and lifted up, and the train of His robe filled the temple." (Isaiah 6:1 NKJV)

After having this vision, Isaiah humbled himself and confessed his sins before God. Later, God called Isaiah to the ministry and Isaiah willingly said: *"Here I am Lord, send me."*

When I was saved at the young age of eleven, I had a "Shekinah glory" experience, meaning I experienced the presence of God. As I came forward to give my heart to Jesus, the atmosphere was so electrifying to me. God's presence was so profuse that the Sanctuary at United Baptist Church in Gobler, Missouri, seemed to be filled with smoke or fog. I was surrounded with a presence that was full of love and peace. That experience was truly transforming; to this very day, I have never wanted to turn back from following Jesus. Having a genuine salvation experience has enabled me to stay focused on Jesus and His plan for my life.

A second way we can stay focused is to "Press Forward" toward the goal that we have written down. One lady told me that she is working toward developing a stronger prayer life. In order to accomplish this, she must guard each day so that nothing can deter her from pressing forward toward God and developing the prayer life that she has envisioned. She has to be deliberate in reserving prayer time to God. Her efforts must become habitual.

One young man said that he wants to grow in spiritual maturity because he is tired of staying at the baby stage of spiritual growth. He said that he is tired of being on milk. However, he admitted that he loses focus easily and turns to the world for answers. With God's help, he is determined enough to take new strides in studying God's Word and attending Bible Study in order to grow spiritually the way he has envisioned. He realizes that he must make it a habit to keep on pressing on whenever troubles come his way.

The word "press" means to push forcefully. Anytime we give birth to something we have to "push." Giving birth to God's plan is for men and women. When we push, we are literally birthing forth the plan and purpose that God has for us. In order to become God's best, we must push forcefully toward our heavenly goal.

The Apostle Paul faced the same problems as all of us in the area of pressing forward. He says in Philippians 3:12 (NIV): *"Not that I have already obtained all this, or have already been made perfect. But I press on to take hold of that for which Christ Jesus took hold of me."*

Paul acknowledges his limitations; yet he realizes that he is a work in progress. He wants his goals to be aligned with the goals that God has for him. In the previous verse, Philippians 3:10 (NIV), the Apostle Paul states his vision by saying: *"I want to know Christ and the power of His resurrection and the fellowship of sharing in His sufferings, becoming like Him in His death."*

Do you want to know Christ? To know Christ means to develop a relationship with Him. It means to yearn to spend time with Him and not complain during times of suffering and difficulty. It is during the storms that we become more like Jesus. The perilous times allow us to die to self.

A third way for us to stay focused is to "Forget the Past." The word "forget" means to send away or to excuse. Just send away those hurt feelings or painful memories that tend to weigh you down. This can only be done by the enabling power of the Holy Spirit who dwells inside of us. We must ask for God's help in forgiving ourselves of disappointments, failures, and short-comings.

Note what the Apostle Paul says in Philippians 3:13 (NIV): *"Brothers, I do not consider myself yet to have taken hold of it. But one thing I do: Forgetting what is behind and straining toward what is ahead."*

Paul had a great deal to leave behind. Before he was converted, he had persecuted Christians. He was a devout Pharisee, and a strict observer of the law. Now that he is under grace, he must send away or excuse his former life style. He cannot let the former things prevent him from moving forward in Jesus.

Jesus is serious about us as Christians being faithful and sticking to our service to Him. He says in Luke 9:62 (NIV): *"No one who puts his hand to the plow and looks back is fit for service in the Kingdom of God."*

These are strong words. Don't you want to be fit for service in the Kingdom of God? Sure. We all do; therefore, we must be steadfast and stay focused on following Jesus with our entire being.

A fourth way to stay focused is to "Reach for the Prize." A prize is a reward for victory. Everybody loves to receive a prize. An eternal prize is to receive our glorified bodies when we get to heaven. Paul verifies this in Philippians 3:14 (NIV) by saying: *"I press on toward the goal to win the prize for which God has called me heavenward in Christ Jesus."*

Hooray! There is a heavenly reward for staying focused on Jesus, our Prize.

Running the Christian race can be discouraging if we lose our focus. We must keep reaching and stretching to obtain what God has reserved for us. The Apostle Paul further explains that we will receive a crown of righteousness. This crown was compared to the wreath that athletes received in Greece for winning athletic events.

In II Timothy 4:8 (NIV), Paul says: *"Now there is in store for me the crown of righteousness, which the Lord, the Righteous Judge, will award to me on that day—not only to me, but also to all who have longed for His appearing."*

I would like to encourage you to run the race to win. Don't give up; hang in there. There are many runners in a race, just like in the Christian race. Only those who persevere to the end will get the prize. Only those whose eyes remain on Jesus will make it to glory. Paul verifies this by saying in I Corinthians 9:24 (NIV): *"Do you not know that in a race all the runners run, but only one gets the prize? Run in such a way as to get the prize."*

In conclusion, developing a habit of vision requires us to stay focused by making conscious efforts to be repetitious in looking ahead to what God has in store for us. We must not allow the struggles of daily living to cause us to swerve off of the path. Practicing vision or looking toward our spiritual goals for twenty-one days should equip us to develop a habit of focusing on God's plan for us on a regular basis. Our ultimate goal is to become like Jesus.

Ways to stay focused are:

- Write the Vision
- Press Forward
- Forget the Past
- Reach for the Prize

ALWAYS PERSEVERE

In order to develop habits of vision, we must persevere. We must hang in there! Perseverance is holding power; it is like mortar for the bricks to our spiritual house. I conceptualize perseverance by looking through a pair of binoculars. Whenever I look through the binoculars everything is magnified and in closer view. Everything I am focusing on is magnified. The same is true when I am tempted to focus on my problems. Whenever troubles surface, rather than looking at my troubles and having them magnified, I put on my spiritual binoculars by focusing on my vision. When I focus on my vision, I stay on the path that God has charted for me. We magnify whatever we focus on at that time. Focus on Jesus and we magnify Him; focus on problems and we magnify our troubles. Any time we turn our focus away from our goal, we jeopardize our ability to persevere.

The word "perseverance" means to remain constant to a purpose in spite of the obstacles or troubles we face. Is perseverance easy for you? Why is it that some people persevere more easily than others? The answer is we must learn to allow our troubles to mold us—conforming us to the image of Jesus Christ.

In James 1:2–4 (NIV), God's word says: *Consider it pure joy, my brothers, whenever you face trials of many kinds, because you know that the testing of your faith develops perseverance. Perseverance must finish its work so that you may be mature and complete, not lacking anything.*

Remember that perseverance is the ability to remain constant during times of testing. So the next time you are experiencing troubles, be joyful. Joy means gladness of heart. We should remember that troubles and hardships serve to develop and mold us. The tough times serve to make us more complete and mature, causing us to look more like Jesus. The more we encounter and endure, the more we are able to persevere when the next storm comes our way.

A friend once told me the story of two frogs who fell into a container of cream. One frog just complained about the situation. It complained that the cream was cold, and how unfortunate for them to be in that situation. This poor frog gave up and perished in the cream. The second frog did not complain. It made the best of the situation by being determined to continue to paddle and think positive thoughts. As the frog swam round and round in that container of cream, the cream became butter. The solid foundation of the butter enabled the frog to leap to freedom and to achieve the life that it was designed to accomplish.

The moral of that story is to persevere, keep on going despite the circumstances. Something good will surface if we don't give up. Good things happen from seemingly bad circumstances. We must be confident, knowing that God has a purpose in whatever we are experiencing.

Hebrews 10:35 (NIV) says: *So do not throw away your confidence; it will be richly rewarded.*

Confidence is one of the keys to perseverance. We must be fully persuaded that God is more than able to do all that He has promised. Confidence is being sure of ourselves in accomplishing our goals. Whenever I am facing a challenge, I realize what God has done for me in the past. Having knowledge of that victory gives me confidence to stand under new trials. We must ask ourselves, "What do I know for sure?"

Immediately, we will answer with responses like, "God is my Deliverer"; He is my Savior"; "He will provide"; or "I know my Redeemer lives." Knowing who God is will ensure our confidence and will keep us motivated to press forward.

Galatians 6:9 (NIV) says: *Let us not become weary in doing good, for at the proper time we will reap a harvest if we do not give up.*

On June 13, 1994, I began H.O.P.E. Outreach Ministries, Inc. (H.O.P.E. is an acronym for Helping Other People Excel). One of the objectives of the ministry was to help men and women in destitute situations to become more self-sufficient. An avenue for achieving this goal was to teach Bible Studies on location in the housing complexes where these individuals lived. Many times I became weary when I didn't see a dramatic change in behavior. I had been taught that when real learning takes place, there is a change in behavior. Therefore, I cried out to God, "Am I making a difference?" I felt like I was pouring out my heart and soul to these people and I wasn't really seeing a noticeable change.

God spoke to me very clearly and said, "Keep your focus on Me!" That command has been a guiding force for my life. My job is to be obedient. God is the one who changes the lives of individuals. One by one, I started to see changed lives in both men and women. Not only were they changing spiritually but they were changing financially and socially. Women began to get off of welfare and attain good-paying jobs that could sustain them and their families. Men and women began to go back to school to complete their G.E.D. (General Educational Development). Some went on to college to obtain a degree that enabled them to acquire a professional career with a better paying job.

God taught me to be obedient in spite of how things appeared around me. I am reminded of the message that the Apostle Paul wrote to Timothy in II Timothy 2:3 (NIV): *"Endure hardship with us like a good soldier of Christ Jesus."*

The word "endure" means to tolerate or to suffer with. We must endure hardships like a good soldier. A good soldier strives to please his or her commanding officer. It must be our heart's desire to please Jesus in all that we do. We model obedience in the lives our own spouses, children, and all those in our sphere of influence. The world is watching us as Christians. Our obedience must mirror that of Christ, who said in John 4:34 (NIV): *"My food is to do the will of Him who sent Me, and to finish His work."*

Don't you want to finish well? It should be our desire to be obedient to the will of God and to finish His work. We must not only finish His work, but we must finish well. In order to finish well, we must be fighters. Life gets hard sometimes, but we must fight like good soldiers, knowing that God has equipped us with all that we need in order to be victorious. Jesus considered doing God's will and finishing His work paramount to His very existence. His very nourishment was to do God's will.

Hebrews 12:1b (NIV) says: *Let us run with perseverance the race marked out for us.*

Every race has a finish line. Perseverance requires us to aim for the finish line without getting off track. There is a course marked out for each of us. We must endeavor to stay on track.

KEEP WAITING

In waiting for the vision, we must guard it, grasp it, and guarantee it. The vision is for an appointed time and it will surely come to pass if we keep waiting. Wait means to remain still until God directs us to move. We keep on serving Him in the capacity that He last instructed us. As we wait, we expect a favorable outcome. In other words, we wait in hope. Hope is the happy anticipation of something good.

I remember when our older son, Charles Jr., was four years old. We told him that we would be going on a softball trip for the weekend. My husband, Charles, was playing on a fast pitch softball team in St. Joseph, Missouri, and we were making plans to go to Cedar Rapids, Iowa. Little Charlie, as we called him, waited so patiently by gathering toys that he wanted to take on the trip; he cleaned his room without being reminded to do so. He was especially well behaved as he joyously talked about the trip. When Saturday morning finally came, he was all smiles. As we traveled, he kept saying, "Mom, are we there yet?" I would respond, "No, but we will be soon."

When we finally arrived, I said, "Sweetheart, we are here!"

He looked around with so much disappointment in his facc and said, "Mommy, I don't see any rabbits."

I said, "Rabbits?" Then I realized what he was saying and I said, "Oh, honey, I didn't say that we were going to see the rabbits. I said that we were going to Cedar Rapids... Cedar Rapids, Iowa."

In his four-year-old hearing, he thought we said "see the rabbits" and we had said "Cedar Rapids." After his bewilderment, he began to cry. My husband then said, "Let's find this boy some rabbits!"

Our son's tears were not tears of manipulation; they were tears of disappointment from a broken dream and, in his mind, a broken promise.

So we set out to find some rabbits before we even checked into our motel. We did this because of his expectation and hope. He had genuinely expected to see some rabbits.

I believe God is the same way with us. When we seek to obey His voice and we wait patiently for what he has promised, He gives our dreams to us. The Bible says that after Abraham had waited patiently, he received what was promised to him, the birth of Isaac (Hebrews 6:15). Abraham waited twenty-five years from the time of the promise of Isaac to the time of Isaac's birth. (Genesis 12:2–4; Genesis 21:5)

In waiting for the vision, one of the things we must do is to guard our vision. Once we have cast our vision forth, we must guard it to protect it from those who will attempt to snatch it from us. We know that Satan is the culprit behind this snatching. For example in Genesis 37:5, Joseph's brothers hated him because he had a dream and told it to them. The passage reads: *Joseph had a dream, and when he told it to his brothers, they hated him all the more.* (Genesis 37:5)

The brothers already hated him because their father, Jacob, had given Joseph an ornamented robe or coat of many colors. The garment was richly ornamented; it was the kind worn by the virgin daughters of kings. This favoritism displayed by Jacob their father heightened the jealousy of the brothers. Joseph's brothers felt that they had a dual reason for hating him. They hated him because he was his father's favorite; now it appeared that he was God's favorite too. So they hated Joseph all the more. Joseph was the eleventh out of twelve sons. These twelve sons later became the twelve tribes of Israel. God had plans for all of the sons, but God's plans for Joseph exceeded them all.

Joseph told his brothers his dream in the following passages:

Genesis 37:6–7, 9 (NIV): *He said to them, "Listen to this dream I had: We were binding sheaves of grain out in the field when suddenly my sheaf rose and stood upright, while your sheaves gathered around mine and bowed down to it." Then he had another dream and he told it to his brothers. "Listen," he said, "I had another dream, and this time the sun and moon and eleven stars were bowing down to me."*

Joseph's brothers and father were outraged! "How could this be?" they thought. Joseph was next to the youngest out of twelve sons. They were wondering why God would choose Joseph. It sounds like Joseph may have been taunting them about his dream, but I believe he was trying to process this overwhelming revelation. Nevertheless, he was not being received well by his family members.

Sibling rivalry is common in families, but what is uncommon is the deep hatred that was manifested by Joseph's brothers. This kind of hatred breeds bitterness, rage, and murder. Joseph's brothers threw him into a pit intending to kill him. Out of a guilty conscience, they retrieved him from the pit and sold him into slavery. In all that Joseph endured, God remembered him because God was with him. What a great place to be in our relationship with God when we can say that God is with us. When God is truly with us, every step is directed and orchestrated by Him.

Our family will not always receive what we are disclosing about our revelations from God. Therefore, we must guard the vision so that no one will dissuade us. Outside voices have a tendency to deter us from the true voice of

God. We must screen the voices that enter our spirit, mind and heart. We must make sure that God's voice is the only voice we are yielding to in our daily walk.

Something else we must do when waiting for our vision to come to reality: We must grasp our vision. Grasp means that we take hold of our vision or internalize it. Have you really taken hold of the vision that God has given you? If we don't grasp our vision by internalizing our dreams, Satan will snatch them from us. I believe that when Joseph was communicating his dream to his brothers, he was trying to internalize it. He was only seventeen years old when the vision was revealed to him by God. Such a dream can be overwhelming for a young teenager. It wouldn't have taken much for the brothers to hate him all the more because they were already jealous of him.

Joseph was thirty years old when the vision came to pass. God's grand design is never hurried; everything worthwhile takes time. God was doing a work in Joseph while he was waiting those thirteen years.

When we wait for the vision, we can guarantee it. We can take it to the bank, as the expression goes. A guarantee is a promise to make good or a firm assurance that the promise will come true. What we must do after the promise is given is believe in it. We must believe that if God said it, we believe it!

In Genesis 42:6 (NIV), the dream comes to reality. It reads: *Now Joseph was governor of the land, the one who sold grain to all its people. So when Joseph's brothers arrived, they bowed down to him with their faces to the ground.*

At this time, the brothers did not realize who Joseph was; they did not know that he was the Prince of Egypt, the second in command to the Pharaoh. Joseph had the power to decide whether they lived or died. He controlled all the food in the land. What a promotion! God said it; we must believe it.

Later on after the disclosure was made, the brothers feared that Joseph would punish them for what they had done to him. They especially became fearful when their father, Jacob, died. Joseph knew their fearful thoughts and had to reassure them. This is what he says in Genesis 50:19–20 (NIV): *But Joseph said to them, "Don't be afraid. Am I in the place of God? You intended to harm me, but God intended it for good to accomplish what is now being done, the saving of many lives."*

God works all things out for good when we obey Him. Everything that happened to Joseph, God permitted. Joseph realized that it was not his brothers who had done those things to him, but God. Our Omnipotent and All-Knowing God had allowed those things to occur in order to groom Joseph for the leadership role that he has now acquired. God used Joseph to save many lives. God's plan was much bigger than what it appeared earlier.

God is the architect of our lives. When we allow Him to do the designing, our building will come forth just fine!

SPEAK RIGHT

The wrong words spoken can distort our vision. We must speak the words that we want to navigate us in the direction of our goal. The right speaking keeps us on track. We magnify whatever we focus on at the moment. Our words become our focus. Negative words will steer us down the wrong path.

For example, have you ever said, "I can't do anything right"?

Imagine the implications of that negative statement. If we do everything incorrectly, then we certainly won't reach our goal. When we speak words like this, our lives tend to go in that direction. A bad day is usually preceded by bad speaking. The Bible says that the tongue has the power of life and death, and those who love it will eat its fruit (Proverbs 18:21). Therefore, we must speak words that have life in them. Our words truly have consequences. I start my day by thanking God for His goodness.

My focus is immediately on God who is good all the time. I realize that as His creation, I am good and, consequently, I will have a good day!

I start my day by saying: *"This is the day that the Lord has made; I will rejoice and be glad in it."* (Psalm 118:24)

I heard someone say once that it is much wiser to choose what we say than to say what we choose. God's Word admonishes us to guard our lips. Proverbs 13:3 (NIV) says: *He who guards his lips guards his life, but he who speaks rashly will come to ruin.*

Our words can do a great deal of damage. I'm sure all of us have been guilty of saying the wrong thing at the wrong time. We should pray for wisdom so that God will give us the right words to say. After we have spoken the wrong thing, it is too late to go back to gather our words.

HOW DO WE SPEAK THE RIGHT WORDS THAT WILL GUIDE OUR VISION?

We must speak in faith. In every situation in our lives, we must be firmly persuaded that God is going to do what He says, and then speak according to what God has said. Jesus says in Mark 11:22 (NIV): *"Have faith in God."* When I am facing hardship, I speak works of faith. I try to speak what God's word says. My faith is built by consistently speaking words of faith.

When I was a senior in high school, I knew that I wanted to go to college. However, there was no money for college. I am from a farming family of fourteen children, and my family did not have a great deal of money. So I began to speak faith. I would tell everyone that I came in contact with that I was going to college. I told them that I would become a teacher. Many times they would say, "Earnestine, how are you going to get the money to go to college? College is quite expensive."

I would always respond, "I don't know, but I know that I am going to college."

I started applying for financial aid my junior year of high school, but I had not heard back from any of the schools. Maybe a few schools did respond, but they didn't offer very much money. My Mom and I began to pray for financial aid to Lincoln University in Jefferson City, Missouri. I wanted to go to this school because my aunt had graduated from this university, and she seemed pleased about this selection. Finally, it was the month of May and I was getting ready to graduate from high school. I began to wonder, "Where is the money?"

Nevertheless, my Mom and I continued to pray for financial aid. My father was praying also. Then, on that special day in May, I received a letter from Lincoln University in Jefferson City, Missouri, stating that I was the recipient of an Academic Presidential Scholarship. This scholarship would pay for all four years of my education. The university had never offered this particular scholarship before this time. The letter stated that I must maintain good grades in order to retain the scholarship. How excited I was to receive this blessing from God. Making good grades was no problem because I loved to study and I was not afraid of hard work. After receiving the letter, I said, "Jesus, you did this just for me."

The Bible says that without faith it is impossible to please God (Hebrews 11:6). I want to please God because He is so good to me. Whenever we love someone, we strive to please them. We must strive to please God with our faith.

We must speak in authority. Authority means to have the power to command. Using the name of Jesus, we literally have the power to command mountains to move or tough situations to vanish. However, it takes faith. Jesus says in Mark 11:23 (NIV): *"I tell you the truth, if anyone says to this mountain, 'Go, throw yourself into the sea,' and does not doubt in his heart but believes that what he says will happen, it will be done for him."*

With the command of God's Word comes the permission for that word to act. The power is on the Word of God. As God's children, we have the authority to use the Name of Jesus and to command God's Word to act in our behalf. Do we believe that we have that kind of authority? If we don't believe, then the mountains won't be moved.

I knew a man who had eight children. He and his wife were sitting at the dinner table troubled over the lack of food to feed this family of ten people. The scarce supply was placed before them. The father knew that it was not enough for everyone. So he prayed this prayer, "Potatoes, I command you to multiply so that my family will have enough food to eat!"

Every time one family member would take potatoes from the bowl, more potatoes would come into the bowl. The bowl of potatoes was never completely consumed. There was enough left because the father and mother had the faith to speak to the mountain of lack of food. They used their authority to command the potatoes to produce more in the bowl.

We have that same authority in the Name of Jesus. Philippians 2:10–11 (NIV) says: *That at the Name of Jesus every knee should bow, in heaven and on earth and under the earth, and every tongue confess that Jesus Christ is Lord, to the glory of God the Father.*

We must speak in ownership. We must believe that we already have what we have asked God to give us. For instance Jesus says in Mark 11:24 (NIV): *"Therefore I tell you, whatever you ask for in prayer, believe that you have received it, and it will be yours."*

If you are praying that God will give you a bushel of corn, don't bring Him a cup. Bring Him the bushel basket because you are believing Him for your bushel of corn. If you are praying for rain, carry your umbrella with you as you leave the house.

My grandparents were great people of faith. I remember on one occasion when visiting my grandparents, there had not been rain for a while; the crops were dry. My grandparents owned many acres of land and rain was crucial. With this in mind, my grandmother went to her bedroom and began to pray for rain. After praying for hours, she entered the room where I was sitting and said, "Stine, go and get my clothes off of the clothesline; it's about to rain."

I said, "Grandma, the sun is very bright and there are no clouds in the sky."

She said, "Don't talk back to me, child, just go and get the clothes off of the clothesline."

Very obediently I replied, "Yes, Grandma."

As soon as I brought the clothes inside, it began to thunder. In just a short period of time, rain was coming down from the sky. I loved seeing my Grandmother's faith working so vibrantly. She took ownership of her request. She had prayed for rain and she acted upon that prayer.

The Bible says in James 4:2b (NIV): *You do not have, because you do not ask God.*

Remember, we must speak what we want God to do for us. We must align our vision up with God's vision and speak what His word says. If we believe, we can receive whatever it is that we ask God for in prayer. Only believe!

Become a Christian

If you don't know Jesus as your Lord and personal Savior and you want to become a Christian, just pray the prayer below. Once you have sincerely prayed this prayer, you should contact your Pastor or some other spiritual leader and make plans to get baptized. Then you are ready to live a life for Jesus!

Sinner's Prayer

Lord Jesus, I am a sinner. Please forgive me of all my sins, and cleanse me from all unrighteousness. I believe that you died for me on the cross and that you rose again. Come now, Lord Jesus, and live your life in me. Fill me Lord, with your Holy Spirit. Thank You, Lord, for saving me. In Jesus Name I pray. Amen.

CHAPTER TWO

THE HABIT OF LOVE

Love is patient, love is kind. It does not envy, it does not boast, it is not proud. It is not rude, it is not self-seeking, it is not easily angered, it keeps no record of wrongs. Love does not delight in evil but rejoices with the truth. It always protects, always trusts, always hopes, always perseveres. Love never fails.

I Corinthians 13:4–8 (NIV)

In building Godly habits, it is essential to build the habit of love. We cannot emulate Jesus without building habits of love. In this chapter, my emphasis will gravitate to acquiring patterns of love. In other words, we will build our love walk. You will remember that it takes approximately twenty-one days to build a habit. I want us to become cognizant of walking the way Jesus walked. Jesus portrayed love in all that He did. He demonstrated a type of love that is called "agape love" in the Greek. The word "agape" means unconditional love—it represents the very nature of God. John

3:16 (NKJV) says: *"For God so loved the world that He gave His only begotten Son, that whoever believes in Him should not perish but have everlasting life."*

The love God rendered toward us was agape love. He sent His Son Jesus to die for us while we were still sinners. We didn't complete any regimen of goodness before Jesus died. He died for us in our sin condition. God sent Jesus to a sin-sick world because God is love (I John 4:8b).

Agape love is known by the actions it prompts. One does not have to stand on a street corner and wear a sign that says, "I love you." Love will be exemplified by the actions rendered toward people. When we truly have a love for all people, giving is automatic. One cannot love without giving.

Sacrificial giving is the nature of agape love. Consequently, one who loves much gives much.

In these last days in which we are living, the love of many will grow cold due to the increased wickedness (Matthew 24:12). We must make great strides to enhance our love walk so that our love won't grow cold. The world will know that we are Christians by our love. I pray that regardless of the offense, we as God's children will be able to respond in a Christ-like manner. Otherwise, our testimony is jeopardized.

LOVE NEVER FAILS

God's love never fails. The word "fail" means to be deficient in or to forsake. People will forsake us but God will never let us down. I know that many people today have been hurt or abused by another person, especially in marriage or in relationships. Because of those hurts, it might be difficult to imagine a God who will not abandon us. We must see God as greater than man; God can do what man cannot do.

It is imperative to understand that God can do anything but fail. God says in Hebrews 13:5b (NKJV): *"I will never leave you nor forsake you."*

My mother once told me of a family member who had mistreated her as a child. On occasion he could have helped the family during hard times, but he chose to neglect her and other family members. When he became ill, she immediately began to make plans to go to the hospital to visit him. I said, "Mom, I thought he had mistreated you when you were a little girl." Her words to me were, "I am not responsible for that. I am not responsible for the way he treated me. I must do what God would have me to do."

I learned a valuable lesson from my mother. We cannot withhold love just because someone mistreats us. We must do the God thing; we must behave in a manner that reflects agape love. In Ephesians 5:2a, the Bible admonishes us to walk in love. The word "walk" means to live in love. In other words, we make love a habit.

Agape love extends even to enemies. In demonstrating God's unfailing love, we must love our enemies. It is natural to love someone who loves us, but it is supernatural to love someone who hates us. Jesus says in Luke 6:27–28 (NIV): *"But I tell you who hear Me: Love your enemies, do good to those who hate you, bless those who curse you, pray for those who mistreat you."*

We need the help of the Holy Spirit to love someone who blatantly hates us.

When I encounter opposition from someone and I know that opposition is motivated by hate, I have to truly pray. At first, I have a hard time when I ask God to bless that person. I feel somewhat hypocritical in my words. But the more I speak the words, the more the words become a reality. We build faith by speaking words of blessing. Eventually, we will believe what we are speaking.

I have witnessed hate in the eyes of people. It is a fearful thing when you know that a person profusely hates you. At first it can be quite demeaning or intimidating. The more I pray the more I realize that the problem lies with the person who hates. I begin to pray for their heart. And simultaneously, I pray that my heart will not develop any bitterness toward the person who hates me. God has taught me to pray until I feel a sense of peace. When I can think about the person without any hurt feelings, I know that God has healed my heart of the hurt. Peace must rule our hearts.

I read a story recently that a lady had a hard time forgiving people and she had a great deal of enemies. One day she was bitten by a dog that was rabid, meaning that the dog had rabies. She went to see a doctor and he told her that she had a few days to live, and she needed to get her affairs in order. She instantly asked the doctor for a piece of paper and she began to write furiously. The doctor then asked her, "Are you making out your will?" She said, "No, I am making a list of all of the people that I am going to bite!"

Although this story is comical, it is representative of people who hold grudges or people who have a difficult time of loving their enemies. We cannot exercise supernatural love without having supernatural power. Loving people who hate us clearly requires the supernatural help of the Holy Spirit.

Loving people who we feel have abandoned us through death requires supernatural power. I am reminded of the story of Naomi in the book of Ruth. Naomi had lost her husband, Elimelech, and her two sons, Mahlon and Kilion. These family members had died after moving to Moab to find a better way of life after being afflicted by famine in Bethlehem. Although Naomi had her daughters-in-law—Ruth and Orpah— in Moab with her, she felt empty, bitter, and desolate. How do we love again when we feel that the situations of life have left us without hope?

Naomi even changed her name to Mara, which means bitter. She told her daughters-in-law to go back to their mothers' home to find a better life for themselves. In Ruth 1:13b (NIV), Naomi says, *"It is more bitter for me than for you, because the Lord's hand has gone out against me!"*

There is no greater desolation than to feel abandoned by God. Naomi felt that God's hand was no longer with her. Have you ever felt that way? We must realize that God is working in our behalf even when we can't see what He is doing. God knows the end from the beginning. Although Naomi was in a bleak state, God was doing something supernatural behind the scenes. He was preparing to catapult Naomi's family into the very lineage of Jesus Christ.

From the tragedy of the death of the men in Naomi's life, Ruth persuades Naomi to allow her to accompany her back to Bethlehem where it was the beginning of barley season. Ruth clung to her mother-in-law. She refused to leave her because of her condition. In going back to Bethlehem, Ruth meets Boaz, a relative of Naomi's husband. Since Naomi didn't have any other sons for Ruth to marry, she eventually met and married Boaz. He became her kinsman-redeemer. Ruth was able to carry on the family name because of Boaz. After she and Boaz became married, they had a son whose name was Obed. Obed was the father of Jesse and Jesse was the father of David. Boaz and Ruth are in the lineage of Jesus. What a miracle!

Because of the selfless love of Ruth, Naomi became full again. God can take us from emptiness to fullness. We must trust his hand. Delays are not denials. Just because we cannot see what God is doing does not mean that he is dormant. We must trust Him at all times and allow his hand to deliver us and make us vibrant.

AFTER GOD'S OWN HEART

Why did God say that David was a man after His own heart? It's paramount to note that David didn't do everything just right. He didn't live a perfectly moral life. So what did David do that was different from his son Solomon and other leaders? David never worshiped any other God but the one true God, the Creator of the universe. God's word says in I Kings 11:4: *As Solomon grew old, his wives turned his heart after other gods, and his heart was not fully devoted to the Lord his God, as the heart of David his father had been.*

You see, David had a heart that was totally devoted to God Almighty. Although he committed many sins, his heart was always repentant and he always humbled himself before the Lord. God considered the fact that David did not worship any other gods.

Wouldn't it be great to be called a person after God's own heart? Our desire must be to please God and to love Him with all of our heart, our soul and our strength. We must repent of our shortcomings and wrongdoings; and we must seek to worship God only. The question should be, "What am I putting first place before God? Is it my job or my material possessions?" God must be our first and foremost love.

Our love must be sincere (Romans 12:9a). Some stories say that the word "sincere" comes from the Latin, meaning "without wax." In ancient Bible days, pottery would develop cracks after setting for long periods of time. Dishonest merchants would put wax over the cracks and sell the pottery as brand new. Honest merchants would guarantee their product by attaching the word "sincere," which meant there were no cracks. The way the customer could test the product was to hold it up to the light. The light would reveal the cracks. The same is true regarding our spirituality. If we want to test a person's love toward us, we can hold it up to the standards of Jesus Christ. His light will reveal any cracks of deception or any false motives.

If we want to be a person after God's own heart, we must clothe ourselves with inward beauty. I Peter 3:4 (NLT) says: *You should clothe yourselves instead with the beauty that comes from within, the unfading beauty of a gentle and quiet spirit, which is so precious to God.*

God looks at the heart, which contains the hidden, inner person. Our outward appearance is irrelevant to Him. Putting on our best suit or expensive jewelry and appearing before God's presence does not impress God. He is looking for that inner beauty that is so precious to Him.

Once I was told a story of a man who was trying to win this woman's heart. He went to her house in a nice suit and drove a fancy car. However, the lady didn't want to have anything to do with him. She kept rejecting him with each visit. This young man decided to write her one letter a day; he thought this would capture her attention. His letter-writing efforts were to no avail; she didn't respond. So he began to write her three letters a day. In all, he wrote her a total of 700 letters. At the end of this ordeal, this young lady married the mailman. The mailman had delivered all of these letters and he was sincere.

Acts 13:22 (NIV) says: *After removing Saul, he made David their king. He [God] testified concerning him: "I have found David son of Jesse a man after My own heart; he will do everything I want him to do."*

God gave this testimony concerning David because he had observed David to be totally devoted to Him. In order to be a person after God's own heart, we must be totally devoted to God and love Him with all of our heart, our soul, and our strength. Deuteronomy 6:5 (NIV) says: *Love the Lord your God with all your heart and with all your soul and with all your strength.*

Jesus says in Matthew 22:37–40 (NIV): *"Love the Lord your God with all your heart and with all your soul and with all your mind. This is the first and greatest commandment. And the second is like it: Love your neighbor as yourself. All the Law and the Prophets hang on these two commandments."*

We must love with our entire being. Love must saturate us. The love walk is not a suggestion, it is a commandment.

LOVE YOUR NEIGHBOR

Have you ever had a neighbor who was difficult to love? Sure, we all have in one way or another. The one question you might ask is: "How do I handle this unusual beast that I call my neighbor?" The resounding answer is "with prayer and love." To love those who love us is natural, but to love those who hate us is supernatural. Therefore, we need the supernatural hand of God to help us in all situations involving our neighbor.

Who is our neighbor? Our neighbor is anyone we can help. It is anyone in our sphere of influence. A neighbor can be a person who lives next door to us or a person who works with us. A neighbor is anyone in our reach that we can impact. Hope Fellowship Church, the church where I am the Pastor, has supported missionaries in Peru, Russia, and Africa. In communicating with these missionaries by Skype, I feel like we are neighbors. In conversing with them face to face through the Internet, they are in our sphere of influence and we are in their reach. A neighbor is anyone that we can reach out to and help.

God's Word says in Leviticus 19:18b (NIV): *Love your neighbor as yourself.*

It seems that we must first love ourselves if we are going to love our neighbor. If we walk around with a negative love image of ourselves, then we are going to have a negative image of our neighbors. We are going to be intolerant of any unusual behavior. Prayer is the key in salvaging any abnormal relationship with our neighbors or our brothers and sisters around us.

Jesus says in Matthew 5:43–45 (NIV): *"You have heard that it was said, 'Love your neighbor and hate your enemy.' But I tell you: Love your enemies and pray for those who persecute you that you may be sons of your Father in heaven."*

I read a story about a Christian man who owned a rice paddy; and his neighbor who was a non-Christian owned a rice paddy adjacent to his. The Christian would rise up early each morning and water his rice paddy. His neighbor would defiantly remove the wooden board that separated the two rice paddies so that the water could flow from the Christian man's field into his own. This continued for a period of time until the Christian could not tolerate it any more. He went to God in prayer because he didn't want to do the wrong thing. God told him to rise up even earlier and water both rice paddies, his and his neighbor's. The Christian was obedient and did as God had instructed him to do. After a few weeks, the non-Christian approached him to thank him for what he had done. He saw an act of kindness that he had never seen. Consequently, the man became a Christian. Praise God! The unsaved neighbor saw Jesus in his Christian neighbor.

Many times we might not want to endure hardships with a neighbor. However, if we can win a brother or sister to Christ, it is worth the struggles.

The ultimate goal is for a soul to be saved.

Jesus tells us that whenever we help one of the "least of these," we are helping Him (Matthew 25:40). Therefore, we need to visit those who are in prison or in the hospital. We need to feed the hungry and clothe the naked. There are so many ways that we can be a neighbor. A good neighbor is one who looks for needs and meets them. I realize that we can't do everything, but we can do our part. Ask God to reveal to you things that you can do to help others. We don't want to be guilty of neglecting Him by neglecting others.

The story of the Good Samaritan demonstrates how we should help our neighbor and who our neighbor is among us. This account is found in Luke 10:30–37. This passage gives three ways we can help someone.

First of all, we can help those who are "**on the way.**" The man who was attacked, robbed, stripped, and left half dead was going down from Jerusalem to Jericho. That distance was seventeen miles of rocky, desert country. Anyone could have been a prey to attackers. This poor man was left on the side of the road. Nevertheless, there were other people who were "**on the way**" to Jericho, among them were a priest, a Levite, and a Samaritan. Both the priest and the Levite passed by on the other side when they saw the half-dead man. Here we have a religious leader and a lay associate who should have demonstrated love and compassion, but they totally neglected to help this man in need.

How many times have we looked the other way because we didn't want to get involved? The Bible tells us in Proverbs 3:27–28 that we should not withhold good from those who deserve it, when it is in our power to act. These two men of God neglected to help when they had the opportunity.

The second way we can be a good neighbor is to help those who are "**in the way.**" The Samaritan did this by entering the injured man's space. When a person is in our space or we are in theirs, we can either step over them or help them. The Samaritan—who was a hated foreigner—chose to help.

Luke 10:33–34 (NIV) says: *But a Samaritan, as he traveled, came where the man was; and when he saw him, he took pity on him. He went to him and bandaged his wounds, pouring on oil and wine. Then he put the man on his own donkey, took him to an inn and took care of him.*

Real love is known by the actions it prompts. The Samaritan displayed genuine love. He did all that was in his power to treat this injured man of his wounds. Then he took the victim to a place where he could be nurtured.

Active love involves sacrifices; it is impossible to love without giving. Those who love much give much.

The Samaritan didn't stop there; he took the next step. He went "**out of the way**" to help. This is the third way we can be a good neighbor. The Bible says in Luke 10:35 (NIV): *The next day he took out two silver coins and gave them to the innkeeper. "Look after him," he said, "and when I return I will reimburse you for any extra expense you may have."*

What a tremendous display of going "**out of the way**" to help someone. Two silver coins were the equivalent of two days' wages and two months in an inn. If there were extra expenses, he committed himself to pay the bill. This Samaritan spent a great deal of money to help a stranger. Jesus wants us to see that this hated foreigner was the one who rendered the help and gave assistance to the man left injured along the road.

Jesus commands us in Luke 10:37b (NIV): *"Go and do likewise."*

We must show acts of compassion like the Samaritan rendered toward this wounded neighbor. He made great sacrifices without thinking of his own well-being or inconvenience. It takes a great deal of love and discipline to perform such kindness. The word compassion means to "suffer with." If we would demonstrate more compassion, we would find ourselves helping people left wounded by divorce, health problems, grief, financial crisis, and day-to-day problems. Many times a listening ear is all a person needs. There are other times when people need more than a listening ear. They need resources. When it is in our power to help, Jesus admonishes us to help. He wants us to be a good neighbor without thinking about the sacrifices. Genuine love involves sacrifices. We cannot love without giving.

I read this story about an elderly woman who was concerned about safety in this ghetto neighborhood. One day she was walking down the streets of this deplorable area and picking up something. Her behavior was quite bizarre and roused police officers to watch her from a distance. They continued to watch this suspicious woman as she would stoop down, pick up something, and hide it in her apron. After watching her for quite some time, the police officers cautiously approached the woman. They asked her to reveal what was in her apron. The lady carefully unfolded her apron, and they saw pieces of broken glass inside. She said that she had noticed all of the broken glass in the neighborhood, and she wanted to pick up the glass so that the children would not hurt their feet.

I thought that this was an act of loving one's neighbor. This elderly woman cared enough for the children in this neighborhood that she wanted to protect them from broken glass. Love is unselfish and sacrificial. Jesus tells us to go and do likewise.

ENCOURAGE YOURSELF

There are times when life can be difficult, but we must encourage ourselves during those times. Friends and family may not always be available to give us encouraging words; therefore we must learn to encourage ourselves. Encouraging ourselves must begin with loving ourselves. Do you love yourself enough to say, "Yes, I can do this!" or "Yes, I am valuable; I do have worth"?

These are statements that must resonate in our minds and hearts if we are going to encourage and motivate ourselves. One Scripture that comes to mind when I need to encourage myself is Psalm 121:1–2 (NIV). It says: *I lift up my eyes to the hills—where does my help come from? My help comes from the Lord, the Maker of heaven and earth.*

When we are discouraged, the answer is to look up! Our help comes from God above. He is bigger and greater than all of our troubles. The greatest tool that Satan uses against us is discouragement. If he can get us to be discouraged, then he has won the battle against us. Discouragement means to lose courage and to be afraid. The battleground is our mind. When Satan can get our minds to feel defeated, then we will believe that we are a failure. Our actions will follow. Everything we do will be unproductive because of the negativity of our words and thoughts. Let's remember the words that God spoke to Joshua when he was taking over leadership of Israel. Joshua 1:9 (NIV) says: *"Have I not commanded you? Be strong and courageous. Do not be terrified; do not be discouraged, for the Lord your God will be with you wherever you go."*

Those are motivational words from our Creator; He says for us to be strong and courageous because our strength comes from Him. So why are we afraid? Let's trust in God in all that He has commanded us to do. We must encourage ourselves.

The word "encourage" means to urge forward or to persuade; it means to counsel; and to put courage in (*World Book Dictionary*).

When we are feeling defeated, we must put courage into ourselves by speaking God's Word. Say words like, *"Greater is He who is in me than he who is in the world"* (I John 4:4b).

Or *"I can do all things through Christ who gives me the strength"* (Philippians 4:13). Speaking the right words helps to build us up in the Lord.

In the Old Testament, David encouraged himself in the Lord his God. David was the commander of the army of Israel. While their families were in Ziklag, the Amalekites came into their camp and took captive all the women, children, and their wives. No one was killed, but they destroyed the camp by fire. When the soldiers found out what had happened to their families, they were talking about stoning David. David wept until he could not weep anymore. Then the Scriptures say that he encouraged himself in the Lord his God (I Samuel 30:6b). After he encouraged himself and prayed to God, all of the children, women, their wives, and livestock were confiscated from the Amalekites with God's help and direction; nothing was missing—young or old, boy or girl, plunder or livestock. Everything was recovered!

In times of crisis, we need to do what Psalm 27:14 (NIV) says: *Wait for the Lord; be strong and take heart and wait for the Lord.*

We must remember that delays are not denials. God has a plan for us if we can only wait for Him. I am reminded about the story of Thomas Edison. Mr. Edison had more than 1,093 inventions. When he was working on the storage battery, he failed to see results after 10,000 attempts. A friend remarked to him, "Thomas, why don't you just give up? Can't you see that you have failed?" Thomas Edison responded to him, "I have not failed. I have just found 10,000 ways that won't work!"

We must have that same kind of tenacity. We must never ever give up when we know God has commanded us to do something.

I am going to give you three things that we must realize in order to encourage ourselves. One thing we need to remember is that we are **temporal.** Temporal means that we are human and we will live only for a time. With that in mind, we must remember God's all-surpassing power that works in us as Christians. II Corinthians 4:7 (NIV) says: *But we have this treasure in jars of clay to show that this all-surpassing power is from God and not from us.*

As humans, we have a great power working inside of us. We are insufficient but God is all-sufficient. Let's rely on His power working inside of us so that He can receive the glory for all the blessings that occur in our lives. Inside of us is a great treasure. We have the Holy Spirit of God living inside of us and the light of the Gospel of Jesus Christ. Knowing this should encourage us because we should realize that the power is not from us. It is from God Almighty. He is our creator and we are the work of His hands.

The second thing that we need to remember is that we are **triumphant**, which means that we are victorious; we are an overcomer and a conqueror. II Corinthians 4:8–9 (NIV) says: *We are hard pressed on every side, but not crushed; perplexed, but not in despair; persecuted, but not abandoned; struck down, but not destroyed.*

No weapons from Satan will prosper against us. When life is pressing in against us, it will not crush us to death. Regardless as to how troubled we may become, we are not hopeless. We may be treated badly by our enemies, but we are not left alone; God will never leave us nor forsake us (Hebrews 13:5b). There may be situations that totally strike us down, but they will not eliminate us. God is in control!

We have the victory because of what Jesus Christ did for us on Calvary. We are more than conquerors. Jesus paid the price for us. His power is at work in us helping us to be triumphant in all that we do.

A third thing that we must realize if we are going to encourage ourselves is that we are **tabernacular.** This word means that we are like a tabernacle; God lives in us. I Corinthians 6:19–20 (NIV) says: *Do you not know that your body is a temple of the Holy Spirit, who is in you, whom you have received from God? You are not your own; you were bought at a price. Therefore honor God with your body.*

We should be encouraged by knowing that the Holy Spirit lives in us. We must guard what we put into our bodies or what we do with our bodies. Years ago there was a popular saying whereby people would say, "It's my body and I do whatever I please." As a Christian, our bodies are not our own; we belong to God. Everything we do or say should bring Him glory and honor.

As I conclude this chapter, let's grow in habits of love by growing more in love with Jesus. Jesus is love and God is love. Becoming more saturated in the love of God will enable us to forebear difficult people. Remember in the last days that the love of many will grow cold. I pray that our love will fuel the entire world, and the light of Jesus will radiate around the globe!

CHAPTER THREE

THE HABIT OF PRAYER

"Ask and it will be given to you; seek and you will find; knock and the door will be opened to you. For everyone who asks receives; he who seeks finds; and to him who knocks, the door will be opened."

Matthew 7:7-8 (NIV)

Prayer is a powerful habit to possess. Where would we be without prayer? Ever since I was a little girl, I have built my prayer habits. Nevertheless, every year I pray and ask God to help me to grow stronger in my prayer walk. I ask the Holy Spirit to be my helper as I seek Him daily for direction and wisdom. The soul without prayer is like lungs without air. Prayer is a necessity for life itself. It is also important to note that when we pray, we must believe. When we believe, we will receive whatever we ask for in prayer. (Matthew 21:22)

God's Word tells us in I Thessalonians 5:17 (NKJV) to *"pray without ceasing."* To pray all the time does not mean that we go around talking out loud to ourselves. Such behavior could reap negative consequences. It does mean that we walk in an attitude of prayer. To pray without ceasing means that God is always at the forefront of our thoughts and actions.

Once a little child was praying and she prayed, "Dear Heavenly Father, bless my mommy and daddy. And dear God take good care of Yourself. If anything happens to you, we're sunk!"

This child knew the power of prayer and she recognized the importance of God in our lives. We know that nothing will ever happen to God, but this little girl is cautioning us in our own relationship with God. If anything ever happened that weakened our own relationship with God, we're sunk—meaning we are in deep trouble!

AFTER THIS MANNER

Jesus teaches us how to pray in Matthew 6:9–13. He gives us the Lord's Prayer as a pattern or model. A pattern is a way of doing something. When we consider the Lord's Prayer, it is personal. We are to replicate it to fit our personal lives and needs.

Jesus first of all tells us how not to pray. He says in Matthew 6:5 (NKJV): *"And when you pray, you shall not be like the hypocrites. For they love to pray standing in the synagogues and on the corners of the streets, that they may be seen by men. Assuredly, I say to you, they have their reward."*

A hypocrite is a pretender, "one who wears the mask." Jesus is saying for us to be sincere. Don't stand in crowds and pray long prayers just to be seen. If we do this, we will not get our blessings. Jesus says that we have already received our reward by the solicited attention that we receive from men.

The following is a definition of prayer:

- A request to God in the Name of Jesus by the aid of the Holy Spirit.
- Drawing near to God.
- Communication with God. (*Vine's Concise Dictionary of Bible Words*)

When we consider these three components, the entire Trinity is involved when we pray—God the Father, God the Son, and God the Holy Spirit.

We pray to God our Heavenly Father; Jesus tells us in Scripture to pray in His Name because He is the Way to the Father. The Holy Spirit helps us to pray because we do not know how to pray as we should; therefore, the Holy Spirit intercedes for us with groans that words cannot express (Romans 8:26).

When we pray, we draw near to God. God says if we draw near to Him, He will draw near to us (James 4:8). It is such a wonderful feeling to move into the throne room of God in prayer. Once I was praying to God and I prayed, "God, give me more of you." And He whispered to me so gently, "Give Me more of you." Those words from God transformed my life.

Prayer is definitely communication with God. We talk to Him as well as listen to Him. Many times God has spoken to me in quiet meditation or He has spoken to me in the quiet hours of the night. The important thing is to develop a relationship with God so that we communicate with Him day or night.

In following the pattern of the Lord's Prayer found in Matthew 6:9–13 (KJV), we must first "**Acknowledge**

God." The word "acknowledge" means to admit the existence, reality, and truth of God; it means to praise God.

Matthew 6:9a (KJV) says: *After this manner therefore pray ye: Our Father which art in heaven.* We can see that our prayers should be directed to God our Heavenly Father. He is distinct from our earthly father. He is also called "Abba" father, which means daddy—a personal relationship.

Matthew 6:9b (KJV) says: *Hallowed be Thy Name.* The word "hallowed" means holy. God's name is holy, which means set apart. God wants us to approach Him by recognizing that His Name is holy; He is a Holy God. Since God is holy, He commands us to be holy. In I Peter 1:16, God says: *"Be ye holy because I am holy."*

Matthew 6:10a (KJV) says: *Thy Kingdom come.* God's Kingdom is the realm in which He rules. We must acknowledge God as being our King. Does He rule in your life? God says in His Word that if we seek Him and His Kingdom, whatever we need will be added unto us (Matthew 6:33). As Christians, the Kingdom is within us (Luke 17:21b). We don't have to go around seeking the Kingdom of God; His dominion is right inside of us.

Matthew 6:10b (KJV) says: *Thy will be done in earth, as it is in heaven.*

God's will is His purpose; it is His desire, determination, and deliberate design for us. Our prayer is for God's will to be done in our lives and not for our own will to be implemented. A man gave an illustration of doing God's will. He used the illustration of a box of crayons. When he was little, he had to decide which color was appropriate for whatever picture he was coloring; he had to also learn how to color within the lines. In doing God's will, we follow those two imperatives. Choosing the right color of crayon is the same as choosing the appropriate step to take in our daily lives according to the will of God. Coloring within the lines is indicative of staying within the confines of God's will for us, not swaying to the right or to the left. We want to do exactly what God wants us to do.

Secondly, in following the pattern in the Lord's Prayer, we must "**Ask God**" for what we need. James 4:2b–3 (NIV) says, *You do not have, because you do not ask God. When you ask, you do not receive, because you ask with wrong motives, that you may spend what you get on your pleasures.*

Many times we are agonizing over not having certain things when we have not asked God for them. Whatever we need we need to present our request to God. Matthew 6:11 (KJV) says: *Give us this day our daily bread.* Our daily bread is whatever we need specifically for that particular day. If we need wisdom, we must ask God for it and He says that He will give it to us liberally (James 1:5).

If we need forgiveness for our sin, we must ask God to forgive us. Matthew 6:12 (KJV) says: *And forgive us our debts, as we forgive our debtors.* Our debts are our sins. Not only do we ask God to forgive us, we must be willing to forgive those who sin against us. Matthew 6:14–15 (NIV) says: *For if you forgive men when they sin against you, your heavenly Father will also forgive you. But if you do not forgive men their sins, your Father will not forgive your sins.*

Forgiving others can be difficult, especially if that person has offended you in an invasive manner. I handle forgiveness by first asking God to help me. Usually I don't experience forgiveness immediately, but I persistently approach God in prayer and ask Him to help me forgive that person of their offense. When true forgiveness occurs, I experience peace. If I face that individual and I feel any unrest, then I have not truly forgiven from the heart. I go back to my prayer closet and ask God to do more healing inside of me. God helps me in this area every time. As Christians, the failure to forgive is detrimental to our spiritual growth. With the aid of the Holy Spirit, we must correct the malady of unforgiveness as quickly as possible so that a root of bitter will not grow inside of us.

As we continue to examine the Lord's Prayer, Jesus tells us how to handle temptation. If we are having difficulty with temptations, we must pray for help. To be tempted is not sin, but to yield to temptation is sin. Therefore, according to Matthew 6:13 (KJV) we must pray: *And lead us not into temptation, but deliver us from evil.*

James 1:13 (NIV) says: *When tempted, no one should say, "God is tempting me." For God cannot be tempted by evil, nor does He tempt anyone.*

God does not tempt us. Satan is the culprit behind all temptations. To be tempted is to be lured into during something that is sinful. According to James 1:13–15, the stages of temptation are:

- Desire or appetite
- Then we are dragged away by our desire or appetite.
- Next, conception occurs. One becomes pregnant with the sin.
- Then one gives birth to sin.
- When sin is full grown, death occurs.

Death is spiritual separation from God.

In the Lord's Prayer, it is concluded by "**Accrediting God.**" "Accredit" means to give credit to God or to honor Him for His attributes; it means to thank God and praise Him. Jesus says in Matthew 6:13b (KJV): *"For Thine is the kingdom, and the power, and the glory, for ever. Amen."*

To truly accredit God is to worship Him or to ascribe worth to Him. He is worthy of our praise. The more we take the time to honor God, the more our own issues will be minimized. We were created to worship God. The Bible says in Revelation 4:11 (NIV): *You are worthy, our Lord and*

God, to receive glory and honor and power, for you created all things, and by your will they were created and have their being.

To grow in our prayer walk is to grow in our praise walk. To praise God for His marvelous acts is prayer. I have a friend who told me that she received more from God by praising Him than asking Him. Sure, God wants us to ask Him for what we need, but to praise Him for what we already have demonstrates great faith.

It is important to set aside a time and place for prayer and praise. There was once an African village that had many converts to Christianity. Those new converts would go through the thickets to find a quiet place to pray. Each convert had his or her own special place to pray. Their constant traveling through the thickets created a path to their place of prayer. Whenever one of the brothers or sisters was neglecting their time in prayer, grass would grow on the path. They would make it a point to confront that person by saying, "Brother, the grass grows on your path."

Are we observant of our brothers and sisters in the Lord so that we can caution them if they are neglecting their prayer life? It is obvious when we neglect to pray because weeds of discouragement, anger, or bitterness grow in our hearts. Let's be diligent in our own prayer lives and hold others accountable when they are neglecting their time with God in prayer.

PRAYER IN TURBULENT TIMES

I am sure you have experienced some turbulence in your life this week. The habit of prayer enables us to pray during shaky times. By being in the habit of praying, we will not turn our attention to substitutes or counterfeits that the world offers. We will automatically pray when troubled times arise.

In James 5:13, God's Word asks a question and gives the answer, *Is anyone of you in trouble? He should pray.* The solution to turbulence is clear; we should pray. Turbulence is a state of agitation or a state of unrest. The problems of life can throw us out of balance or jolt us to a level of emotional disturbance. Prayer is a tool that can help stabilize us. When we are in prayer, whatever shakes us up will not shake us apart. Prayer does not change God, it changes us. God is already stable and at rest. When we pray, we move into God's presence and His peace envelops us.

We are living in perilous times. Disaster and destruction appear to be all around us and they intensify every day. Bad news at times can be the order of the day. Nevertheless, we must remember that God is bigger than our troubles. He is the Captain of our ship.

This story was told to me about a ship that was sinking. The captain asked if anyone aboard the ship knew how to pray. One man stepped forward in great confidence and said, "Captain, I know how to pray." The captain responded by saying, "Wonderful! You pray while the rest of us put on our life jackets. This ship is sinking and we are one life jacket short."

Have you ever felt like your ship was sinking and you didn't have a life jacket? Even if you knew how to swim, you knew at that moment that you needed extra gear; you needed ammunition that was not available. Your troubles were so insurmountable that you were depleted of answers. It is in times like these that we must allow God to be God. He specializes in making a way out of no way. Just call upon Him and watch Him provide a solution.

The Bible tells us in the Book of Jonah about a man who was in a turbulent situation. His name was Jonah, and he was actually running from God because he didn't want to preach to the people of Nineveh. He was being rebellious and didn't think these people needed forgiveness of their sins. God dealt with Jonah through turbulence. In running from God, Jonah boarded a ship headed for Tarshish. However, the men aboard knew that Jonah was in rebellion to God and they threw him overboard.

While overboard, the Lord provided a great fish to swallow Jonah, and he was inside the fish for three days and three nights (Jonah 1:17). Even in Jonah's rebellion, God was still in control of Jonah's life. Jonah recognized God as being the Lord of His life and the God of this turbulent situation. Therefore, Jonah prayed.

Jonah 2:1–2 (NIV) says: *From inside the fish Jonah prayed to the Lord his God.* He said: *"In my distress I called to the Lord, and He answered me. From the depths of the grave I called for help, and you listened to my cry."*

We must remember that nothing can separate us from God's love or His presence. When Jonah prayed, God answered him. In Jonah 2:10 (NIV) it says, *And the Lord commanded the fish, and it vomited Jonah onto dry land.*

The word vomit means to eject forcefully. I believe when we pray, God will catapult us forward toward His purpose for our lives. Jonah later preached the Word to the people of Nineveh and all of them repented. The city of Nineveh was populated with over 120,000 people. What a great harvest of souls.

PRAY FOR HEALING

We live in a fallen world. Sickness at one time or another will come upon all of us. Praise be to God that He has given us power to receive healing! All we have to do is call upon the name of the Lord. Exodus 15:26b (NIV) says: *"I am the Lord who heals you."* God clearly declares Himself as the healer. He is our Jehovah Rapha—the Lord our Healer. God's name is "I AM," which means that He will be whatever we need Him to be for us. When we are sick, He is our healer.

God provided a way for our healing through the cross. When Jesus died for us on the cross, He paid the price for our healing. I Peter 2:24 (NIV) says: *By His wounds you have been healed.* I believe this means total healing—spiritually, physically, mentally, and emotionally. In whatever way we need healing, the blood of Jesus covers our sickness.

Whenever I am sick, whether it is a cold or a stomach ache, I focus on the cross. I seek Jesus and His Kingdom. Matthew 6:33 (NIV) says: *But seek first His kingdom and His righteousness, and all these things will be given to you as well.* We must want Jesus more than we want the healing.

Once I had strep throat and I was very sick with a high fever. The doctor told me that it would take about three days to recover. This particular Saturday morning, I got in bed and turned on my praise music. I was determined that my thoughts would be on Jesus and His goodness. I asked Jesus to heal me, and I praised Him throughout the day. By early evening, I was 100% better. I was able to cook supper for my family and I went to church the next day. I returned to work on Monday totally healed. I knew Jesus had healed my body and I give Him the glory for it.

Whenever we are praying for a healing, we must remain **hopeful.** Hope is confident expectation of good. We must anticipate the healing and trust God to give the positive results. We must be willing to accept His timing. The healing might not come right away, but God has promised to heal us. I know you might ask the question, "What if he doesn't heal me?" We must remain hopeful and keep the faith. Even if God in His infinite wisdom does not provide the healing, we must remain faithful. God is still a good God. He will give us the peace and comfort to endure.

I knew a lady who had cancer and she was not healed of her illness. The family prayed for a healing with faith and hope, but death was the end result. Many people said that God did not answer their prayers. However, He did answer their prayer. Heaven is the ultimate healing. God took her to heaven where she received her glorified body. She will never be sick again. In the meantime, God healed this lady's family by bringing them closer to Him. They began to serve God in a more devoted manner.

Whenever we are praying for a healing, we must remain **humble.** To be humble means that we have lowliness of heart or that we surrender ourselves to God. When we remain humble, we will accept whatever outcome God has for us with a trusting heart.

James 4:10 (NIV) says: *Humble yourselves before the Lord, and He will lift you up.* Worshiping and praising God are ways that we can humble ourselves before Him. Focus on God and seek His Kingdom first. If the healing doesn't come quickly or if it doesn't come at all, then God will give us His peace. Regardless of the outcome, God must be glorified. He is still a sovereign God and He is still faithful.

Whenever we are praying for a healing, we must expect **hearing** from God. Hearing means that we are expecting God to listen and to respond favorably to our request. We must have faith that God is going to reply with healing. We must believe that God will hear our humble cry. A cry to God is a plea for help. When David had sickness in his body, he called to God and God healed him. Psalm 30:2 (NIV) says: *"O Lord my God, I called to You for help and You healed me."* In this passage, David is giving us a public testimony regarding his healing.

When I was growing up, my parents would sing a song with the following words:

> *I love the Lord, He heard my cry.*
> *He pitied every groan.*
> *As long as I live troubles will arise.*
> *But I hasten to His throne.*

In my older years, I have come to cherish these words. Troubles and sickness will come upon us in this life. We have a God that we can run to for help. God hears our cry and He answers us with His healing power. My faith is unrelenting. I never stop believing that God will do the miraculous. Jesus is here with us so that the Father may be glorified through Him. Jesus wants us healed; God is honored when we are made whole in spirit, soul, mind, and body.

PRAYER OF REPENTANCE

When we consider making prayer a habit, the prayer of repentance should be constant. We must be cognizant of things that are offensive to our Lord. When we love someone, we try our best to please them. Jesus, our Lord and Savior, is worth pleasing and honoring to the utmost.

It is a good idea to do introspection—an internal examination with the objective of improvement. Only the Holy Spirit can do a thorough job of seeing on the inside of us and making the necessary corrections. As a Christian, we should desire to throw away everything that prevents us from serving God.

Hebrews 12:1 (NIV) says, *Let us throw off everything that hinders and the sin that so easily entangles, and let us run with perseverance the race marked out for us.*

There is a race marked out for us as God's children. Sin can delay or prevent the completion of that race. We must get the sin out of our hearts. A common misconception among believers is that we can **add** Christ to our lives and not **subtract** sin. In order to truly repent, we must add Christ and subtract sin with the help of the Holy Spirit. Sin and Christ cannot coexist. The blood of Jesus cleanses us from all of our sins.

Something we can remember about sin is that it takes us farther than we want to go; we stay longer than we want to stay, and we pay more than we want to pay. A good repentance prayer is the prayer that David prayed in Psalm 139:23–24 (NIV). It says: *"Search me, O God, and know my heart; test me and know my anxious thoughts. See if there is any offensive way in me, and lead me in the way everlasting."*

What a humble prayer to utter. When we pray this prayer, we are inviting God to thoroughly examine us so that we can be a better person. This prayer indicates that we want to be heaven-ready.

<u>Repentance means:</u>

- To have Godly sorrow
- To confess the sin
- To turn from the sin
- To turn to God (*Vine's Concise Dictionary of Bible Words*)

Once there was a little boy who had made a total mess of his room. His mother scolded him and demanded that he clean his room. After his mother left the room, he prayed to Jesus this prayer: "Dear Jesus, I'm sorry that I made such a mess of my room today. But I sure had fun doing it!"

As long as we enjoy the sin, we will never truly repent. We must feel sorry for the wrong act; and with all of our heart, we must desire to change. Sin means to miss the mark or to disobey God. God is just a prayer away. He stands ready to forgive us and cleanse us from all unrighteousness whenever we sin. I John 1:9 (NIV) says: *If we confess our sins, He is faithful and just and will forgive us our sins and purify us from our all unrighteousness.*

No sin is out of God's reach for forgiveness. David was full of pride, greed, self-righteousness, and lust. He committed adultery and he was a murderer. The list goes on and on. Nevertheless, after he committed adultery with Bathsheba and had her husband killed, he prayed the following prayer, *"Have mercy on me, O God, according to Your unfailing love; according to Your great compassion blot out my transgressions. Wash away all my iniquity and cleanse me from my sin."* (Psalm 51:1–2 [NIV])

What sin have you committed? All you have to do is confess it. Perhaps for years, you have been harboring guilt and shame. Jesus paid the price on Calvary to free us from condemnation. Freedom is a by-product of repentance. Whenever we repent, freedom follows. John 8:36 (NIV) says: *So if the Son sets you free, you will be free indeed.*

CHAPTER FOUR

THE HABIT OF NEWNESS

Therefore, if any man be in Christ, he is a new creature: old things are passed away; behold, all things are become new.

II Corinthians 5:17 (KJV)

Building habits of newness should become just as prevalent as building any other Godly habit. We will remember that a habit is a pattern of behavior acquired through repetition. One must desire to acquire habits of newness. Whenever Jesus comes into our heart, we are a new person. The habits of the old person will not apply.

Have you ever purchased a new cell phone? You have to get used to the features of the new cell phone. What you did with the old phone will not work for the new one. The same is true concerning developing habits of newness; the things we did in the old nature will not work for the new.

God's Word says in II Corinthians 5:17 (NIV): *Therefore, if anyone is in Christ, he is a new creation; the old has gone, the new has come!*

The key word in that Scripture is to be "in" Christ. We must become a part of the family of Christ. Since we are in His family, we have His DNA. Therefore, we will look like Christ and walk like He walked. When Christ is "in" us and we are "in" Him, our nature will be new and our demeanor will be new.

There was a little girl who asked her mom a very important question. She asked, "Mommy, is it true that Jesus lives in us?" The mother answered, "Yes, that is true."

The little girl continued her curiosity by asking, "Mommy, is it true that Jesus is so much bigger than we are?" The mother replied, "Sure, dear, Jesus is so much bigger than we are." Then the little girl exclaimed, "Then, Mommy, shouldn't He show through!"

The statement is profoundly true. Jesus should show through all of us who profess to be Christians. The character of Jesus will innately radiate through us when we are indwelled by the Holy Spirit. We can't make ourselves become new. Whenever we force our newness, our change does not last. I have seen many new Christians try to force their newness; they rush ahead of the work of the Holy Spirit. In just a short time, they begin to backslide or slip into the patterns of their old nature. They usually don't persist for the long haul. Instead, they gradually migrate back to the old friends and the old way of living.

DRINK NEW WATER

In order to be new, we must drink from the fountain that God has made available for us. The fountain contains new water—the Holy Spirit.

Have you ever had any bad water? Bad water can cause sickness and death.

In a sense, Adam and Eve had bad water in the Garden of Eden when they ate of the forbidden fruit; they disobeyed God. Eating the forbidden fruit had the same consequences as drinking bad water. Disobedience is an act of sin, and sin produces death because it separates us from God. The bad water of disobedience brought about death. Jesus entered the world to bring us good water of life to drink. The water that Jesus provides will give us eternal life.

Sin entered the world through the one man, Adam. Righteousness entered the world through the one man, Jesus Christ (Romans 5:12–15). As I embrace this revelation, the sin that Adam and Eve committed is the same as drinking bad water and sin came upon us all. Jesus has come to give us a fresh drink of living water.

Revelation 22:17b (NIV) says: "*Whoever is thirsty, let him come; and whoever wishes, let him take the free gift of the water of life.*"

Are you thirsty today? Are you spiritually in a dry place where there is no water? Jesus invites you to come to Him and take a fresh drink of water. It is free! There is no charge for this unspeakable gift. We did nothing to deserve such a priceless treasure.

Titus 3:5 (NIV) says: *He saved us, not because of righteous things we had done, but because of His mercy. He saved us through the washing of rebirth and renewal by the Holy Spirit.*

The phrase "washing of rebirth" means regeneration. The following is the definition of "regeneration":

- New Birth; to be born again
- Spiritual change from old to new nature
- Restore to right relationship with God
- Act of God through the Power of the Holy Spirit (*Vine's Concise Dictionary of Bible Words*)

Whenever I see the word regeneration, I immediately think of the word "generator," which is a power source. When we are regenerated, we have a new power source—the Holy Spirit. In I Peter 1:23 (NIV), God's Word says: *For you have been born again, not of perishable seed, but of imperishable, through the living and enduring word of God.*

It is God's imperishable seed that makes us children of God. His seed makes us born again spiritually. Since the seed of God is on the inside of us, we can call Him "Abba, Father," which means "daddy," a personal relationship.

In order to receive the new water of the Holy Spirit, we must: <u>Yearn for It.</u>

The word "yearn" means to desire earnestly. In the account of the Samaritan woman at the well, Jesus knew that the woman was yearning for Him. For this reason He said that He earnestly needed to go to Samaria. In His journey from Judea to Galilee, He didn't have to go to Jacob's well to pursue this forlorn woman. Nevertheless, He did. He sought her out showing no partiality or discrimination.

The Bible says in John 4:7, 9 (NIV): *When a Samaritan woman came to draw water, Jesus said to her, "Will you give Me a drink?"*

The Samaritan woman said to Him, "You are a Jew and I am a Samaritan woman. How can you ask me for a drink?" (For Jews do not associate with Samaritans.)

This is an illustration of how Jesus will seek us out. He shows no regard to race, creed, gender, or nationality. The

Samaritan woman was thinking of excuses why Jesus should not be talking to her. She did not realize that she was Jesus' mission.

In John 4:10–11 (NIV), Jesus responded to the Samaritan woman by saying:

"If you knew the gift of God and who it is that asks you for a drink, you would have asked Him and He would have given you living water."

"Sir," the woman said, "you have nothing to draw with and the well is deep. Where can you get this living water?"

There are parallel events occurring in this scene. The woman was concerned about an instrument to draw the water, and she was also concerned about where she can get the living water. Her moral situation was deep and she was in need of the living water that Jesus was offering.

In receiving the new water, the Samaritan woman must: <u>Yield to It.</u>

Yield means to surrender. In John 4:13–15 (NIV), we see that she is yielding to what Jesus is presenting to her. Jesus answered: *"Everyone who drinks this water will be thirsty again, but whoever drinks the water I give him will never thirst. Indeed, the water I give him will become in him a spring of water welling up to eternal life." The woman said to him, "Sir, give me this water so that I won't get thirsty and have to keep coming here to draw water."*

To reach deeper into the woman's heart, Jesus asked her to go and get her husband. She replied to Jesus that she had no husband. Jesus told her that she had answered correctly. In reality, she did not have a husband. She had been married five times and the man she was living with was not her own husband. This could mean that she was sleeping with someone else's husband, or she was living with this man out of wedlock. Whatever the case, she was clearly not married to the man with whom she was living.

Jesus did not address her in a condescending manner. He continued to show love and compassion. Jesus' mission was to save her soul. He wanted her to come to know Him as her Lord and Personal Savior. As a result of Jesus' approach, the woman genuinely yielded to Him.

Once we receive the new water that Jesus offers, we must: Yell with It.

Yell means to shout out. In John 4:28–30, 39, and 42 (NIV), we see the Samaritan woman yelling with the Good News. The passage says: *Then, leaving her water jar, the woman went back to the town and said to the people, "Come, see a man who told me everything I ever did. Could this be the Christ?" They came out of the town and made their way toward Him. Many of the Samaritans from that town believed in Him because of the woman's testimony, "He told me everything I ever did." They said to the woman, "We no longer believe just because of what you said; now we have heard for ourselves, and we know that this man really is the Savior of the world."*

We can attest that because of the woman's testimony, many came to know Jesus as Savior and Lord. When others can witness a change in us, they will be convinced that Jesus is real. They must see that we have wholeheartedly changed; then they will be willing to seek Jesus out for themselves. Generally speaking, everyone wants something bigger than they are and they want to experience something grand. Let's take the Gospel of Jesus to others. The Holy Spirit will do the drawing and mighty things will happen.

NEW SHOUT OF VICTORY

Since Jesus died for us on the cross, we have a new shout of victory. Sure, troubles come to us in this world but Jesus says that He has overcome the world. In John 16:33b

(NIV), Jesus says: *"In this world you will have trouble. But take heart! I have overcome the world."*

The word "overcome" means to prevail against or to win. If we truly believe that Jesus has already prevailed over the world, why do we take the weight of the world on our shoulders? No doubt just this week some of you may have felt overtaken by the world's system. There is no system or power that can prevail over the power of God. He is omnipotent, omniscient, and omnipresent. Nothing can surpass these attributes.

There was a man who had been ill, so he went to see a doctor. The doctor called him back into his office for a consultation and he gave him the following diagnosis: "Mr. Jones," he said, "I have bad news and worse news to give you."

Mr. Jones replied, "Give me the bad news."

The doctor responded, "I regret to tell you but you have 24 hours to live."

Mr. Jones stated in a dejected way, "If that is bad news, I can't imagine what the worse news can be."

The doctor hesitantly said, "I forgot to tell you yesterday."

That story might cause us to chuckle. What about when life gives us a blow? How do we respond? Regardless as to what the circumstance might be, we have the victory. The victory is won on our knees. We must pray without ceasing; therefore, when the trials and troubles come, we have already won the battle.

The definition of the word victory is to lead in triumph or to defeat an enemy in a battle. This means that we are above our circumstances and not under them. Jesus causes us to triumph because of the victory that we have in Him. II Corinthians 2:14 (NIV) says: *But thanks be to God, who always leads us in triumphal procession in Christ and through us spreads everywhere the fragrance of the knowledge of Him.*

As Christians, we walk around with the fragrance of Christ, which is a sweet aroma of His presence. There is something different about the demeanor and glow of a Christian. That glow emits the presence of God.

In order to demonstrate a new shout of victory, we must allow the Holy Spirit to untie our ropes. Untie means to loose or unfasten. It means to be free. How are you in bondage? We can be in bondage through past hurts, unforgiveness, or sinful habits. I used to be in bondage by my low self-esteem. I had a low sense of worth; therefore, I was constantly feeling inferior, feeling that I couldn't do things as well as others. Jesus broke that bondage by the power of the Holy Spirit. God showed me that He did not create me as an inferior and that I could do whatever He called me to do. That revelation changed my life and I will never be the same. I am always rising to higher heights.

STAND IN FREEDOM

When we are made new in Jesus, we are free. We are not bound by old sinful habits. Jesus says in John 8:31–32 (NIV): *"If you hold to My teaching, you are really My disciples. Then you will know the truth, and the truth will set you free."*

The key to freedom is to hold to the teachings of Jesus. The Word of Jesus is our road map. Whenever we digress off course, we become lost. Pride will persuade us to continue on the wrong path because we will try to solve the problem ourselves. Have you ever been traveling with someone and you told them they were lost? The first thing they usually say is, "I know where I am." In actuality, you know that they are lost. Not admitting that we are lost is a sure sign of failure. It is that kind of bullheadedness that keeps one from getting on the right path. We cannot afford to be stubborn with Jesus. We must hold to His teachings by obeying His Word.

We must be obedient to the teachings of Jesus Christ. As disciples, we are learners and followers of Jesus. Once we root ourselves in Jesus, we will know the truth and the truth of Him will set us free. To know Jesus means to come into relationship with Him. We know Jesus by spending time with Him and by abiding with Him.

Jesus taught me that I was created for a purpose. Having that knowledge, I realize that I am free to accomplish whatever God has called me to accomplish. It is "knowing the truth" that sets us free. Jesus is truth. Our knowledge and our relationship with Him release us to greatness. God's word says in John 8:36 (NIV): *"So if the Son sets you free, you will be free indeed."*

Freedom means that we are free from all chains; we are free from whatever binds us. Galatians 5:1 (NIV) says: *It is for freedom that Christ has set us free. Stand firm, then, and do not let yourselves be burdened again by a yoke of slavery.* We must stand firm and not let Satan take our freedom away from us. Satan desires to steal from us anything that exalts Jesus. We must stand firmly on the word of God.

To be bound by sin is to be burdened by a yoke of slavery. A yoke is defined as:

- Wooden frame fitted around the necks of a pair of oxen to harness them.
- The condition of being under another's power. (*The World Book Dictionary*)

From this definition, one can see that sin is a yoke of slavery. Our rights are restrained. When sin is our master, it is Satan who is ruling us. We want to do right but, instead, we find ourselves doing wrong.

Jesus says in Matthew 11:29–30 (NIV): *"Take My yoke upon you and learn from Me, for I am gentle and humble in heart, and you will find rest for your souls. For My yoke is easy and My burden is light."* Our union with Jesus is light. The Holy Spirit inside of us guides us to true freedom. It is no longer our desire to sin; our desire is to please our Master. The Holy Spirit helps us to live a Christ-centered life.

Just because we are free does not mean that we can do what we like. I Peter 2:16 (NIV) says: *Live as free men, but do not use our freedom as a cover-up for evil; live as servants of God.* Because we love Jesus, we should not jeopardize our relationship with Him by sinning. We are free because of the price He paid for us on Calvary. Jesus died and shed His blood so that we can be free through the forgiveness of our sins. Without the shedding of blood, there is no forgiveness of sins (Hebrews 9:22).

CHAPTER FIVE

THE HABIT OF FAITH

Now faith is being sure of what we hope for and certain of what we do not see.

Hebrews 11:1 (NIV)

"I tell you the truth, if you have faith as small as a mustard seed, you can say to this mountain, 'Move from here to there' and it will move. Nothing will be impossible for you."

Matthew 17:20 (NIV)

Are you considered as the "righteous"? The Bible says that the righteous shall live by their faith (Habakkuk 2:4). This Scripture means that if you are born again, you should be developing habits of faith and thus living by faith. You might ask, "How do I build habits of faith?" One should build habits of faith the very same way that any other habit is built; habits are built by repetition. We must practice what we preach. If we say we believe in Jesus and if we tell others to believe in Jesus, then we must demonstrate actions of belief. Worry and doubt cancel out belief. Individuals around us must see that we truly believe in our Jesus by the lifestyle of faith we exhibit.

Jesus says in Matthew 17:20 (NIV): *"I tell you the truth, if you have faith as small as a mustard seed, you can say to this mountain, 'Move from here to there' and it will move. Nothing will be impossible for you."*

A mustard seed is the size of a pencil point. When we consider how small a pencil point is, having faith the size of a mustard seed appears to be an easy task. The power is in the seed, not in the size. Every seed has DNA of the parent plant. The small mustard seed has the potential to grow strong and tall because of its parent plant. The seed of Jesus in us has the potential to grow into strong fruit of faith. This faith will have the ability to move mountains and nothing will be impossible to us. Faith is our belief system. The stronger our belief in the ability of God to do what we speak, the more of God's power is released. Our faith becomes the command that releases the power of God on our behalf.

Hebrew 11:6 (NIV) says: *And without faith it is impossible to please God, because anyone who comes to Him must believe that He exists and that He rewards those who earnestly seek Him.*

Jesus is our King. No one approaches a king without gaining his favor. In approaching Jesus, we must please Him with our faith by believing that He exists. When Jesus sees our faith, He automatically grants what we are requesting of Him. Sure, the answer is sometimes delayed, but He always answers. Delays are not denials.

FAITH WHEN JESUS IS SILENT

How do we respond when Jesus is silent? When we are presenting our petition to Him and He says nothing, how do we respond? We keep standing. We do not make one move until we hear from Him. Our patience is a test of our faith. If we really believe that He exists, then we will be willing to wait for His response regardless of how long it takes.

When Jesus called me to enter the ministry, I was still teaching in the public school system. Many times I would begin to get restless because I knew that Jesus had called me to preach the Gospel, and I knew it would be in a different setting than the conventional classroom. I remember on one occasion I prayed to Jesus, "Lord, I don't want to miss the call that is upon my life. I am getting restless because You are taking so long to respond."

Jesus answered me and said, "Since I called you, will I let you miss it?"

I knew by that response that Jesus is Sovereign and that my life is in His hands. I made a promise to my Lord that I would not make one move until I heard from Him. I kept that promise. I waited a total of fifteen years from the time Jesus called me until the time that I left the teaching profession. When the voice of Jesus said, "It's time now," I had no hesitation. I knew that I was under the guidance of the Holy Spirit and that the call of God was upon my life.

A family member sent me the following quote: "When you are going through something hard and wonder where God is, remember the teacher is always quiet during a test."

Jesus is my Teacher and I have learned to wait for Him. Waiting for God is always a crucial time of testing. The more we trust Him, the more we will be willing to wait on Him, even if we can't see what He is doing. Hebrews 11:1 gives the perfect definition of faith. It says, *"Now faith is being sure of what we hope for and certain of what we do not see."* We are not going to always see what God is doing in our lives. However, all we need to do is believe in Him.

Here are some other definitions of faith:

- Faith comes from the Greek word *"pistis,"* which means a firm persuasion that God is going to do what He says. (*Vine's Concise Dictionary of Bible Words*)
- This word also signifies "Amen," which means "so be it." When God makes a promise, we can say "Yes" and "Amen." (II Corinthians 1:20)
- Belief without seeing. We walk by faith not by sight. (II Corinthians 5:7)
- Trusting in God or relying on God.
- Having complete confidence in God.
- Faith is always active because it is based on our relationship with God. Delayed faith is disbelief.
- Faith is essential for salvation. Ephesians 2:8–9 (NIV) says: *For it is by grace you have been saved, through faith—and this not from yourselves, it is the gift of God—not by works, so that no one can boast.*

Our faith is essential for salvation. Many years ago, I was ministering at an apartment complex where I was visiting ladies from my Bible Study class. I met a girl who was telling me that she was getting baptized at her church. She was about twelve years old. I asked her, "Aren't you excited about inviting Jesus into your heart and becoming a Christian?"

She responded, "I am getting baptized so that I can join the church. No one told me about inviting Jesus into my heart. All I was told is that I was going to be joining the church."

This disturbed me greatly. I then explained to her that salvation involved more than "joining the church." Sure, I know that when we are baptized we are baptized into the family of God. But there is something that must happen on the inside; there is something that must precede joining the church. The missing ingredient here is the transforming experience that occurs when we invite Jesus into our heart through faith by His saving grace. We are saved before the water baptism even occurs. Water baptism is an outward testimony as to what has already happened inwardly. I took her to Romans 10:9–10 (NIV), which says: *That if you confess with your mouth, "Jesus is Lord," and believe in your heart that God raised Him from the dead, you will be saved. For it is with your heart that you believe and are justified, and it is with your mouth that you confess and are saved.*

We prayed the Sinner's Prayer together and she invited Jesus into her heart. At that moment, she was truly born again. A few days later, she was baptized at her church, and after many years, she is still serving the Lord faithfully.

How do we grow in our faith? Romans 10:17 (NIV) says: *Consequently, faith comes from hearing the message, and the message is heard through the word of Christ.* The word "hearing" means to listen with the intent to obey. When you hear the word of God, do you listen with the intent to obey what is said? When we receive the word of God with a heart of obedience, faith grows. We must allow the word of God to take root in our heart, and we must guard that word so that Satan will not steal it. Faith comes by hearing God's word and by putting that word to practice.

Having a relationship with Jesus is paramount if faith is going to grow. Spending time with Him and allowing the word of God to be watered in our heart will enable our faith to blossom.

There was a lady in the days of Jesus who was a Gentile from the region of Tyre and Sidon, a city in Phoenicia. This region is modern-day Lebanon. The lady was a Canaanite woman. The Bible says in Matthew 15:22–23 (NIV): *A*

Canaanite woman from that vicinity came to Him, crying out, "Lord, Son of David, have mercy on me! My daughter is suffering terrible from demon-possession." Jesus did not answer a word. So His disciples came to Him and urged Him, "Send her away, for she keeps crying out after us."

Imagine the faith of this desperate Canaanite woman! She is not a Jew. Gentiles were despised by Jews; they were considered as dogs. Nevertheless, she had the courage and faith to approach Jesus with a request to heal her daughter. Somewhere she had to hear the Gospel in order for her faith to grow to such magnitude.

The conversation between the Gentile woman and Jesus becomes more demeaning. Jesus says the following in Matthew 15:24 (NIV): *"I was sent only to the lost sheep of Israel."*

I feel that this statement is devastating to a mother who comes in a state of helplessness because her daughter is being tortured by demons. What we must realize is that Jesus is only testing her faith. Jesus is sent to all nations of people, regardless of race, gender, age, or economic status. The woman demonstrates perseverance. Matthew 15:25–27 (NIV) says: *The woman came and knelt before Him. "Lord, help me!" she said. He replied, "It is not right to take the children's bread and toss it to their dogs." "Yes, Lord," she said, "but even the dogs eat the crumbs that fall from their master's table."*

The Canaanite woman gives a great comeback of faith! She is willing to settle for crumbs! Her faith amazes Jesus. Jesus was testing her and she passed the test with flying colors. Because of her faith, Jesus granted her request. Matthew 15:28 (NIV) says: *Then Jesus answered, "Woman, you have great faith! Your request is granted." And her daughter was healed from that very hour.*

Jesus honors our faith. He tells us how to get our prayers answered. In Matthew 7:7–8 (NIV), He says, *"Ask and it will be given to you; seek and you will find; knock and the door will be opened to you. For everyone who asks receives; he who seeks finds; and to him who knocks, the door will be opened."*

This Scripture is indicative of the Canaanite woman. She persevered in her faith. She continued to ask, seek, and knock and her request was granted. God Himself promises that whenever we seek Him with all of our heart, we will find Him. Jeremiah 29:13–14 (NIV) says, *"You will seek Me and find Me when you seek Me with all your heart. I will be found by you," declares the Lord.*

FAITH TO SEE JESUS

We must have enough faith that urges us to want to see Jesus. We must have the kind of faith whereby we want to climb higher in our walk with the Lord. In Isaiah 6:1 (NIV), Isaiah says: *"In the year that King Uzziah died, I saw the Lord seated on a throne, high and exalted, and the train of His robe filled the temple."*

Isaiah had a vision of God being high and lifted up. This experience superseded any experience that he had ever encountered. He saw God in a manner that was incomprehensible. This vision of the excellence and supremacy of God caused Isaiah to repent of his sins. Later when God called him, he responded by saying, "Here am I Lord, send me." (Isaiah 6:8)

We need to see Jesus with spiritual lenses. Jesus wants to disclose more of Himself to us. Nevertheless, we must hunger for Him. We must desire to partake of more of His essence.

Definition of the word "see":

- Comes from the Hebrew word *"ra'ah"* (*Vine's Concise Dictionary of Bible Words*)
- To perceive or understand
- To get acquainted and to know

- To have a vision—spiritual revelation
- To experience

In Psalm 119:18 (KJV), the Psalmist says: *Open my eyes, that I may see wondrous things from Your law.* This must be our prayer and our heart's desire. We must urgently want God to open our spiritual eyes that we may climb to greater depths in Him. In this quest for spiritual depth, we must fix our eyes on Jesus because He is the Author and Finisher of our faith (Hebrews 12:2). Our faith begins and ends with Jesus. He is the one who gives us the faith to climb higher.

I have learned that it takes effort and determination to climb higher to see Jesus. One must thirst and hunger for more of Jesus. Jesus says in Matthew 5:6 (NIV): *"Blessed are they which do hunger and thirst after righteousness: for they shall be filled."* Jesus gives us more of Himself when we have the faith to yearn for more of Him. To receive more of Jesus is to "see" Him.

In reading the story of Zacchaeus in Luke 19, it is apparent that he wanted to see Jesus and Jesus wanted to see him. Therefore, Jesus put it on His agenda to see Zacchaeus on His last trip to Jerusalem as He passed through Jericho. Zacchaeus desired to experience the presence of Jesus. The word "presence" means to be where Jesus is.

In Luke 19:2–4 (NIV) it says: *A man was there by the name of Zacchaeus; he was a chief tax collector and was wealthy. He wanted to see who Jesus was, but being a short man he could not, because of the crowd. So he ran ahead and climbed a sycamore-fig tree to see Him, since Jesus was coming that way.*

The name Zacchaeus in the Hebrew and Greek means pure and righteous. Zacchaeus is everything but what his name says. He is deceptive and greedy. As a tax collector, he had cheated many people out of money, and this is why he was hated by the Jews. His wealth was at the expense of the Jewish people. Zacchaeus' name represented what he would become, not what he currently was as a tax collector. Zacchaeus ran to climb the sycamore-fig tree so that he could receive a name change. He overcame the obstacle of his height by climbing a tree that gave him the height he needed in order to see Jesus. When we want to see Jesus, we will climb to any height in order to accomplish our goal. Our faith will enable us to persevere and receive our touch from Jesus.

Despite our reputation, Jesus is able to transform our behavior. We are all made new after the hand of Jesus touches us. Jesus is able to make something beautiful out of the most deplorable person. In order for Zacchaeus to be transformed, he had to "position" himself for his blessing. He needed to be in the right place. Luke 19:5–6 (NIV) says: *When Jesus reached the spot, He looked up and said to him, "Zacchaeus, come down immediately. I must stay at your house today." So he came down at once and welcomed him gladly.*

Jesus reached the right position for Zacchaeus to see Him. Zacchaeus exercised prompt obedience and came down out of the tree immediately.

Jesus had a divine appointment with him. This trip was Jesus' last trip to Jerusalem before His Crucifixion; He was crucified shortly thereafter. Zacchaeus was one of the last people that Jesus ministered to before He was crucified.

We are all important to Jesus. He will go out of the way to see us saved.

Jesus stands at the door of our heart waiting for us to receive Him. The door must be opened from the inside. We must let Jesus into our heart; He will not force Himself inside our spiritual house. Revelation 3:20 (NIV) says: *"Here I am! I stand at the door and knock. If anyone hears My voice and opens the door, I will come in and eat with him, and he with Me."*

In the process of inviting Jesus into our heart, there must be "penitence." Penitence means sorrow for sinning or doing wrong; it also means repentance.

Luke 19:8–9 (NIV) says: *But Zacchaeus stood up and said to the Lord, "Look, Lord! Here and now I give half of my possessions to the poor, and if I have cheated anybody out of anything, I will pay back four times the amount." Jesus said to him, "Today salvation has come to this house, because this man, too, is a son of Abraham."*

An indication that Zacchaeus had been transformed internally is demonstrated in his ability to make restitution. He was willing to give half of his possessions to the poor, and he was willing to repay four times the amount to the people he had cheated. Such generosity indicated Zacchaeus' true repentance. When there is genuine repentance, our actions will prove it.

We are on Jesus' agenda just like Zacchaeus was at the very mind and heart of Jesus. Luke 19:10 (NIV) says: *For the Son of Man came to seek and to save what was lost.* The word "seek" means to look for intently and diligently. The word "save" means to rescue. Jesus is looking for us diligently in order that we may be rescued from sin. Once we receive Jesus as our Lord and Savior, we must tell others. Jesus wants to spend eternity with us in heaven.

FAITH TO MOVE MOUNTAINS

As a reminder, Jesus says that if we have faith as small as a grain of mustard seed, we can say to the mountains in our life to move from here to there and they shall move; nothing shall be impossible for us (Matthew 17:20).

Whenever we have faith as small as a mustard seed, we will climb higher to see Jesus and we will climb higher to see Him in all situations in our lives. There are times when troubles will be so insurmountable in our lives that we will feel helpless. Despite the mountains, Jesus is able to move them. Our faith must prevail. I can remember a time during my years in college when I needed money. I had received a four-year academic scholarship, but I still needed money for miscellaneous items and special school supplies. I prayed and asked God to help me. Since I was a freshman in college, I did not want to get a job my first year. Just the newness of college life and the study requirements were more than I could handle for the first year.

I prayed in faith that God would move the mountain of financial lack in my life. A few days later, I went to my mailbox and received a letter from a nearby church. This letter began by saying that I had been selected as their "Daughter of the Year." This was a ministry within the church whereby each year this organization would select a college student that they would bless financially for one year. By the hand of God, they had received my name as a candidate. I was invited to attend their church for a special luncheon and for recognition as their newest recipient of this award. After the luncheon, I was given a money tree with varying amounts of bills—$5, $10, $20, and so on. I had never seen such showering of money! Thereafter, I received money for my birthday, holidays, and other times throughout the year to demonstrate acts of kindness.

Whenever I have a need in my life, my mind journeys back to this work of God. I saw God's hand intervening to bring about this blessing. He truly moved the mountain of financial lack and I know He will move any mountain that is placed in my path. All I have to do is believe. The same is true for you. What mountain are you facing right now? It does not have to be financial; it can be in your marriage or other relationships; it can be sickness; or it can be an addiction. Whatever the mountain is, believe that God will move it. A mountain is something that is insurmountable without God's help. The Bible says that we can have whatever we ask for in prayer, if we believe (Matthew 21:22).

We can even speak to the mountain by quoting Scriptures. The following are some of the Scriptures that I quote and make personal:

Philippians 4:13 (KJV)—*I can do all things through Christ who strengthens me.*

Philippians 4:19 (KJV)—*But my God shall supply all my needs according to His riches in glory by Christ Jesus.*

Isaiah 54:17 (KJV)—*No weapon that is formed against me shall prosper; and every tongue that shall rise against me in judgment I shall condemn. This is the heritage of the servants of the Lord, and my righteousness is of the Lord.*

Deuteronomy 28:13 (KJV)—*And the Lord shall make me the head, and not the tail; and I shall be above only, and not beneath.*

I Peter 2:24 (KJV)—*By His stripes I am healed.*

I John 4:4 (KJV) —*Greater is He who is in me than he who is in the world.*

Psalm 139:14 (KJV)—*I thank God that I am fearfully and wonderfully made.*

Hebrews 13:5b (NIV)—*"Never will God leave me and never will He forsake me."*

As we speak to the mountain in faith, three things will happen:

There will be "**Shifting.**" The word "shifting" means to move from one place to another. The atmosphere will shift because we have spoken to the mountain. God's word brings about a change in the atmosphere. The greatest change must occur in our heart. Doubt must be removed from the heart and a shift will occur. Mark 11:23 (NIV) says: *I tell you the truth, if anyone says to this mountain, "Go, throw yourself into the sea" and does not doubt in his heart but believes that what he says will happen, it will be done for him.*

The key is to have faith in our heart and not doubt. Doubt is the opposite of faith and, therefore, cancels out our faith. God says we are double-minded when we possess doubt in our heart; He says we are unstable in all of our ways and our prayers will not be answered. Let's exercise our faith by speaking words of faith and watch the atmosphere change.

The Bible says in Proverbs 18:21 (KJV) that death and life are in the power of the tongue. The tongue is a powerful tool. We should speak blessings instead of curses. Let's be careful about the negative words that proceed out of our mouths, especially to our children. There was once a mother who was always speaking negatively to her son. She told him words like, "You will never make it in life; you are impossible." One day this little boy, who was in third grade, went to school. The teacher gave them a writing assignment. She asked them to write an essay about what they wanted to be when they grew up. This little boy responded in his paper, "I just want to be possible. My mom is always telling me that I am 'impossible.' Teacher, I just want to be possible."

What chilling words! These statements are indicative of the effect of negative words. Our words truly have the power of life and death.

A second thing will happen when we speak to the mountain in faith. There will be **"Shaping."** The word "shaping" means to form or to mold. The power of God's word will shape us. God created the heavens with the spoken word. Psalm 33:6 (NKJV) says: *By the word of the Lord the heavens were made, and all the host of them by the breath of His mouth.* Just imagine the entire universe was created when God said, "Let there be." Whatever God wanted to appear, He spoke by His creative power. Hebrews 11:3 (NIV) says: *By faith we understand that the universe was formed at God's command, so that what is seen was not made out of what was visible.*

God made something from nothing. He spoke it and it came into being.

As we speak God's word over our lives, creative things will happen to us. God will give us beauty for ashes. God's word says in Isaiah 61:3 (NIV): *To bestow on them a crown of beauty instead of ashes, the oil of gladness instead of mourning, and a garment of praise instead of a spirit of despair.*

Just speak the word of God, and we will be transformed and our status will change.

By God's creative power, He shapes us through our circumstances. Romans 8:28 (NIV) says: *And we know that in all things God works for the good of those who love Him, who have been called according to His purpose.*

Whatever experiences we may have in our lives, God uses them to shape us.

A third thing will happen when we speak to the mountain in faith. We will be "**Shouting.**" Shouting means to make a loud cry or to have a voice of thanksgiving. When God answers our prayers, we should begin to shout. Psalm 47:1b–2 (NIV) says: *Shout to God with cries of joy. How awesome is the Lord Most High, the great King over all the earth.* Words cannot fully describe the goodness of our God.

Psalm 105:1 (NIV) says: *Give thanks to the Lord, call on His name; make known among the nations what He has done.* We should always share our testimonies about the goodness of God. His blessings are unlimited. Our testimonies help to build faith in others. No testimony is too small or insignificant. A testimony is like a mustard seed; when we plant it into the hearts of others, great things happen!

CHAPTER SIX

THE HABIT OF OBEDIENCE

"If you love me, keep My commands."

John 14:15 (NIV)

Developing habits of obedience involves love. Jesus says that if we love Him, we will obey what He commands. Love manifests itself in obedience. Love and obedience involve the component of loyalty. I am reminded when we purchased our first puppy. He was a true example of obedience. However, he did not start out obeying us. He grew in obedience as his love and devotion for us grew. In other words, he developed the habit of obedience because of the internalization of love.

We named our dog Big Foot because of his enormous feet. He was part collie, part chow, and part German shepherd with blackish-gray fur that literally gleamed in the sunlight. As he grew and frolicked through the back yard day by day, we very quickly noticed his loyalty to the family. Every time we pulled up into the driveway, he rushed to the fence to greet us. Then he would quickly dash to the back door so that we could let him inside the house. After he was left alone all day, he readily awaited a gentle stroke on the head or mild rubbing on the tummy. Without fail, Big Foot remained faithful. He looked forward to our fellowship and companionship with one another.

When we consider the obedience of Jesus, He said in John 4:34 (NIV): *"My meat is to do the will of Him that sent Me, and to finish His work."* Jesus made it clear that He was here on a mission. His love for God kept Him focused. Nothing or no one could distract Him from that mission—the mission of winning lost souls to Him.

As I parallel our obedience to Jesus and the obedience of our dog, Big Foot, I am reminded of how food offered to our dog by a neighbor still did not deter him from responding to our presence. On one occasion, our next door neighbor was feeding Big Foot a delicious bone that he was immensely enjoying. When my husband and I drove up in our car, Big Foot quickly and unabashedly abandoned the bone and headed for the front door to greet us. The neighbor was quite crushed by the dog's rash behavior and remarked, "I thought Big Foot liked me, but when any of you guys come around, he acts like I don't exist."

Of course we apologized to our neighbor for our dog's behavior; she could see the loyalty and devotion of Big Foot toward his family members. She came to understand that whenever family members arrived home, her time with Big Foot would cease.

Just like with our dog Big Foot, God wants us to have loyalty and devotion toward Him. God is our Master; He is our Lord. He wants us to treat Him like He is our master. In order to do this, we must surrender our all to Him. Romans

12:1 (NIV) says: *I beseech you therefore, brethren, by the mercies of God, that ye present your bodies a living sacrifice, holy, acceptable unto God, which is your reasonable service.* There's no greater joy than to arise each morning and say, "Lord, Have your way in me today."

Many times people remark to me, as a Pastor and an outreach minister, that they are afraid to totally surrender to God because they are afraid of what He might ask of them. He might ask them to go to some remote part of the world where they do not wish to go. He might ask them to quit their job and send them to another job that they don't like. Rest assured: God will not send us anywhere that He has not already prepared us. God gradually unfolds His plans to us and readies our heart for them. Therefore, when it is time to embark upon His good and perfect will, we should be ready to obey by saying, "Here am I, Lord, send me!"

OWNERSHIP

Just as in the case with our dog Big Foot, bringing him home sealed the ownership. He was invited into our space, an atmosphere of love and warmth. God invites us into His space and He wants us to invite Him into ours. This occurs simultaneously when we invite Jesus into our heart. Revelation 3:20 says: *"Here I am! I stand at the door and knock. If anyone hears my voice and opens the door, I will come in and eat with him, and he with me."*

I received Jesus into my heart to be my Lord and Savior at the age of eleven. It was at a revival service at United Baptist Church in Gobler, Missouri. The evangelist from Chattanooga, Tennessee, preached an electrifying message and then gave the invitation. I went forward and cried out to Jesus to come into my heart. It was at that moment that

I knew I was born again. The atmosphere that evening was infiltrated with the glory of God's presence. It was tangible and powerful! I know that God is real and I have walked in that assurance ever since that night.

My father and mother, Thomas Bob Ross and Mary Anna Ross, played a great part in my salvation. My father had explained to me that if I wanted Jesus to come into my heart that all I had to do was invite Him to come and live inside of me. So I prayed the sinners' prayer with my father in the dining room of my grandparents' home. I remember fresh country air blowing through the window as the sheer curtains swayed in the wind. That day holds unforgettable memories and fragrance for me. After I prayed the sinner's prayer with my father, the light in the room seemed brighter and my joy was unspeakable. The revival service that evening was a culmination of what had begun when we had prayed the sinner's prayer earlier that evening.

On the night of the revival service, the choir was melodious and the response from the congregation was thunderous. The move of Holy Spirit was like nothing that I had experience. It was an atmosphere in which I wanted to remain. I was reminded of Peter, James, and John when they were upon Mount Transfiguration in Matthew 17:1–13. They wanted to build a tabernacle so that they could dwell in that place forever. My salvation was sealed by the indwelling power of the Holy Spirit. God says in His Word that He set His seal of ownership on us, and put His Spirit in our hearts as a deposit, guaranteeing what is to come (II Corinthians 1:22).

Since I know that God owns me, I truly seek to please Him. I long to worship at His feet and drink from the fountain of His presence. My heart's cry every day is "Speak Lord, your servant is listening; what do you want me to do today?" Having an attitude of obedience requires listening to God's voice and distinguishing His voice from the multitude of voices that surround us each day. Obeying my parents at the age of eleven was a great deal like obeying the Lord. It was predicated upon love and the desire to please the one I love.

When we consider ownership, Jesus paid the price for us with His blood.

What a true friend! He loved all of us so much that He came down from heaven to die for us. Jesus first of all demonstrated loyalty to His Heavenly Father by obeying Him in coming to earth. Once He arrived, He completed the assignment from God in dying for our sins. We can exemplify loyalty to our Heavenly Father by obeying His every command. What has God commanded you to do today? Have you obeyed that command? The greatest demonstration of our love for the Master is to obey Him. John 14:15 (NIV) says: *"If you love Me, you will obey what I command."*

Ownership involves commitment. When I invited Jesus into my heart, I realized that He was mine and I was His. I didn't want to do anything to jeopardize our relationship. I'm reminded of owning a doll collection when I was twelve years old. My commitment was demonstrated by the care that was rendered to those dolls. Their hair was well combed; they were in a sufficiently preserved place so that others couldn't handle them without my permission. I kept that doll collection until I left home for college, at which time I rendered the entire collection to one of my younger siblings.

Being committed to that doll collection taught me a great deal about responsibility. Those dolls were not only items that I could enjoy during times of play, they were entities that had been entrusted to my care. God cares for me; I am entrusted to His care. I am His and He is mine. He will never leave me or forsake me (Hebrew 13:5b).

DEVOTION

Devotion means to be dedicated to the Lord. Matthew 16:24 (NIV) says: *"If any man will come after Me, let him deny himself, and take up his cross, and follow Me."* Jesus makes it clear what He expects of us if we are going to be truly devoted to Him. We must first deny ourselves. To deny ourselves is to renounce any selfish motives and align our motives with the will of God. To take up our cross is to suffer for our Lord; it is through suffering that we grow into the image of Jesus. To follow Him is to obey His commands and follow the path He that he has laid out for us.

Big Foot was devoted to the family. When any one of us—my husband, our sons, Charlie Jr. and Andrew, or myself—appeared in his presence, no one else mattered. I have observed him as he abandoned treats and pats on the head from neighbors just to be with his family. Our presence to him was a call for his attention.

Devotion comes with a price. When one is devoted, that individual dies to self. Their will becomes the will of the person to whom they are devoted. The paramount ingredients of devotion are love and loyalty. God called me to the ministry when I was staying home during my six-year maternity leave from teaching. When God called me in 1979, our older son, Charlie Jr., was only a year and a half old. My first thought was, "Lord, our son is so young. How can I leave him and go into the ministry?" God reassured me that this was not the time to enter the ministry. I made Him a promise that I would not make one move until I heard from Him. Our second son, Andrew, was born three years later. My time at home was a training ground as a parent and as a Christian getting equipped to enter the ministry. After six years of staying home as a young mother and wife, I returned to the teaching profession. With each new day, I waited to hear from God concerning His instructions for me to enter full-time ministry. Nevertheless, God did not give me the "green light" to leave teaching until fifteen years later from the time that He called me.

As I waited those fifteen years, great things happened in the teaching profession that equipped me for ministry. In the 1991–92 school year, I was named the St. Joseph Missouri Teacher of the Year and the Missouri State Teacher of the Year. This honor opened many doors for me to travel and share creative teaching ideas. As I traveled throughout various parts of the United States, each day I was reminded of my call to full-time ministry. Although I was reaching thousands of people, this was not the call that God had for me. This was training ground. Each day of teaching, I was vigilant and prayerful. I remained mindful of God's call on my life. I was not running from God, I was waiting for Him to say, "It's time." On many occasions, I would say, "Now, God, don't let me miss your call on my life." God reassured me that since He had called me, He would not let me miss His call.

Then, the time finally came. It was a season of restlessness. I felt as if I were pregnant with an overflow of God's call inside of me. I literally heard God's voice inside of me say, "It's time now. I release you to go and do what I have called you to do." After waiting fifteen years, I entered full-time ministry on June 13, 1994. I kept my promise to wait until I heard from God. When God first called me, He said, "Feed my sheep. Do the things that Jesus did; you know what to do, just do it!"

I remember saying to Jesus, "But, Lord, I don't know what to do." Jesus then replied, "Do what I have already put inside of you to do." Being reminded of those instructions, I started an outreach ministry doing those things that God had taught me in the teaching profession. God informed me that He had called me to a bigger classroom—a classroom of teaching and preaching His Word. He wanted me to reach people with the Gospel and win lost souls for Him.

ASSIGNMENT

Stepping out into the ministry and leaving the teaching profession was like giving birth to a child. Those years of waiting were like a gestation period. The call was growing inside of me. My final year of teaching was like a time of labor because I felt God's hand drawing me from the classroom and birthing forth something new. The new life that began was H.O.P.E. Outreach Ministries, Inc., which was founded on June 13, 1994. H.O.P.E. is an acronym for "Helping Other People Excel."

Leaving the teaching profession was purely an act of obedience. I thank God for my faithful husband, Charles, and our two sons—Charles Jr. and Andrew—who supported me 100%. Having my family by my side made this transition easier. Many of my teaching colleagues didn't understand why I would leave such a promising profession. My career was quite productive and blessed. I was only forty-one years old, which was really the prime of my life.

I first started the ministry by reading with children at apartment complexes. I had no books or money. So I checked out every Bible-based book from the libraries in St. Joseph, Missouri. My emphasis was on spreading the Gospel through reading. The donations began to flow in when people realized that I was serious. Pretty soon we were reading at four different apartment complexes and three nursing homes. We averaged reaching 700 children a month and 500 elderly residents a month. My motto was "Where God guides He provides."

My objectives for reading with the children and the elderly were to break down generational barriers; to promote literacy; to build relationships; to foster volunteerism; and to break down socioeconomic, cultural, and denominational barriers.

In using my gifts of preaching and teaching, I have been invited to speak at church worship services, retreats, and seminars in many cities and states. In past years, I have ministered overseas three times. I have preached in Guatemala, Venezuela, and the Bahamas. Knowing that the call of God was on my life, I began credentialing for ministry from Global University in Springfield, Missouri. I completed all three levels of ministry—Certified, Licensed, and Ordained. After studying for three years, I was ordained in 1999.

Listed below are some of the past or present activities of H.O.P.E. Outreach Ministries, Inc.:

- Summer reading at apartment complexes
- Day camp for disadvantaged children and youth
- Interaction with the elderly involving students from local schools
- Adoption of families for Thanksgiving, Christmas, Easter, and other holidays
- Adult literacy for adults
- Bible Studies in nursing homes, apartment complexes, the YMCA, and other community facilities
- Women's retreats and seminars in various states and locations
- Working with children and youth in the Noyes Home for Children
- Reading and interacting with residents at the Home for the Blind
- Weekly radio and television ministry

I am currently the Pastor of Hope Fellowship Church, Inc., which I founded on June 4, 2009, with the help of my husband, Charles. In establishing this church, we are able to encompass the mission of H.O.P.E. Outreach Ministries, Inc. in spreading the Gospel of Jesus Christ. The outreach ministry and the church work closely together to accomplish God's purpose for our lives. We are a nondenominational church, and we are growing each week. With a strong emphasis on outreach, we reach people from various backgrounds and cultures. We have a wide spectrum of people in our congregation, where all are welcome!

The Mission Statement for Hope Fellowship Church

Our mission is to proclaim the Gospel of Jesus Christ so that others may know Him and make Him known through Evangelism, Worship, and Discipleship. This mission statement guides our lives spiritually in such a manner that we are able to become fully devoted followers of our Lord and savior Jesus Christ. Consequently, others who witness our example will be able to become fully devoted followers of Jesus as well.

CHAPTER SEVEN

THE HABIT OF FAITHFULNESS

Moreover it is required in stewards, that a man be found be faithful.

I Corinthians 4:2 (KJV)

In building Godly habits, the habit of faithfulness is paramount in developing our relationship with God. Wouldn't it be wonderful if all Christians naturally exhibited faithfulness in their service of God? The heartbeat of faithfulness is being saturated with faith in God to the extent that we innately obey His will. We walk around saying, "Yes, Lord."

Are we in the habit of keeping our promises to God and others? If we don't keep our promises to God, then we won't keep our promises to one another. A person who cannot be trusted is considered to be flaky and shaky. God does not want us to be flaky and shaky Christians. He wants faithfulness.

The definition of the word "faithful" is:

- Reliable and trustworthy
- Full of faith in God
- Based on relationship (*Vine's Concise Dictionary of Bible Terms*)

All of us are in some kind of relationship. Everyone wants faithfulness from the ones they love. Without faithfulness, we cannot be trusted. Have you ever wondered if God can trust you? Are you reliable and trustworthy?

God's word says in the New Living Translation of Proverbs 28:20a (NIV): *The trustworthy person will get a rich reward.*

The rich reward will be received in this lifetime as well as in heaven. God honors the faithfulness of His people. One of the things that God requires of all Christians is to be faithful stewards. In fact, God demands our faithfulness as stewards. In I Corinthians 4:2 (KJV), it says: *Moreover it is required in stewards, that a man be found faithful.* In the NIV version of the same Scripture, it says that a steward must be proven faithful. Everything that we do will prove our faithfulness.

Have you ever done any baby-sitting? As a baby sitter, you were a steward. The baby didn't belong to you; the child or infant was only entrusted into your care. Even as parents, our children are not our own; they belong to God.

Psalm 24:1 (NIV) says: *The earth is the Lord's, and everything in it, the world, and all who live in it.* Nothing in this world belongs to us. We have no reason to become prideful because God owns it all. Many times people will boast about their riches when in actuality those riches are on loan to them. They will have to give an account of how they are managing those riches.

The definition of a "steward":

- Manager of someone else's property
- Someone given a trust
- Will have to give an account (*Vine's Concise Dictionary of Bible Terms*)

The entire concept of stewardship is to understand that Jesus is coming back. He has placed us in charge of His property and He is returning to see how we are managing His property. Jesus says in Luke 12:47 (NIV): *"That servant who knows his master's will and does not get ready or does not do what his master wants will be beaten with many blows."*

Those who are faithful stewards will be rewarded in the Judgment Seat of Christ mentioned in Romans 14:10 (NIV), which says: *"You, then, why do you judge your brother or sister? Or why do you treat them with contempt? For we will all stand before God's judgment seat."* Revelations 20:11–15 says that unfaithful stewards will be punished in the Great White Throne Judgment.

Romans 14:12 (NIV) says: *So then, each of us will give an account of himself to God.* God will judge us on the use of our time, talent, and treasures. Are we responsible stewards in managing these three components that encompass the work that God has called us to accomplish? We must be about our Father's business.

MANAGING TIME, TALENTS, AND TREASURES

We must take charge of this trust with the authority granted to us. The Parable of the Talents that Jesus told in Matthew 25:14–30 explains how we need to proceed.

The parable begins by saying in Matthew 25:14–15 (NIV): *Again, it will be like a man going on a journey, who called his servants and entrusted his property to them. To one he gave five talents of money, to another two talents, and to another one talent, each according to his ability. Then he went on his journey.*

This parable is symbolic of Jesus as the "master or man going on a journey." Jesus has entrusted all of us with gifts and abilities according to our capacity to manage them. Jesus will not require anything from us that He hasn't already put in us. He has already equipped us with the ingredients needed to bring about a yield. We as stewards are required to produce an increase.

Every gift is individualized. I Peter 4:10 (NIV) says: *Each one should use whatever gift he has received to serve others, faithfully administering God's grace in its various forms.*

We need to evaluate ourselves to see if we are implementing the time, talent, and treasures that have been entrusted to us. Jesus is coming back again, and He wants us to be rapture ready. If we are faithful in whatever stewardship obligation we have been entrusted, then we will be ready for our Lord's return.

Are we faithful with a little amount of responsibility? If we are faithful with a little amount of responsibility, then we will be faithful with many responsibilities. Luke 16:10 (NIV) says: *Whoever can be trusted with very little can also be trusted with much, and whoever is dishonest with very little will also be dishonest with much.*

We must make strides to multiply our time, talents and treasures. Multiply means to increase in number, amount, and degree.

Matthew 25:20, 22 (NIV) says: *The man who had received the five talents brought the other five. "Master," he said, "you entrusted me with five talents. See, I have gained five more." The man with the two talents also came. "Master," he said, "you entrusted me with two talents; see, I have gained two more."*

We see increase with both servants. Both of them went forth and provided a yield with their investment based upon their own individual abilities. Jesus requires our very best with what we have been provided. Our Master will not compare us with anyone else; He will expect from us what he has demanded from us as individuals.

The other servant who had been entrusted with one talent was not obedient. He hid his talent. Jesus says in Matthew 25:18 (NIV): *But the man who had received the one talent went off, dug a hole in the ground and hid his master's money.* In Matthew 25:28–30 (NIV), the master responded, *"Take the talent from him and give it to the one who has the ten talents. For everyone who has will be given more, and he will have an abundance. Whoever does not have, even what he has will be taken from him. And throw that worthless servant outside, into the darkness, where there will be weeping and gnashing of teeth."*

We see in this parable that the one with the ten talents was given more. Our Lord honors faithfulness; He wants us to increase with great abundance. The servant with the one talent lost what he did have and was punished severely. This punishment is referring to the Great White Throne Judgment during the end of time where the wicked will be punished. The righteous will be rewarded in the Judgment Seat of Christ.

Our primary objective as Christians is to glorify and magnify our Savior. Frequently, I make it a practice to quote the following Scripture in order to keep my focus on God. The Scripture is found in I Peter 4:11(NIV) and it says: *If anyone speaks, he should do it as one speaking the very words of God. If anyone serves, he should do it with the strength God provides, so that in all things God may be praised through Jesus Christ. To Him be the glory and the power for ever and ever. Amen*

FAITHFUL WITH THE WORD

Have you ever wondered about your faithfulness with the word of God? Typically, we take for granted our relationship with the word of God just like we take for granted our relationship with those close to us. God's word deserves faithfulness in complying with its demands.

The leading cause of divorce is a lack of faithfulness and commitment. If we fail to be faithful with those in our close proximity then we will be unfaithful to God. Our Master deserves our trustworthiness; after all, isn't He faithful to us? Being faithful with the word of God means that we are going to use God's word for His glory to bring about the purpose that He intended. It means that we are going to be trustworthy and reliable with the word of God and that we are going to exercise our faith to the fullest.

I once imagined that someone had given me a bag of gold nuggets. I asked myself, "How will I use this valuable treasure?" My mind immediately was consumed with excitement and unlimited possibilities. I had a myriad of ways that I could use this treasure and be faithful with it. Our faithfulness to God deserves that same kind of excitement and anticipation. God's word is the greatest treasure of all; the supply is unending and the power of it is insurmountable. The treasure of God's word can be taken to heaven with us whereas earthly treasures remain here on earth and will fade away.

Hebrews 4:12 (NIV) gives us a definition of God's word. It says: *For the word of God is living and active. Sharper than any double-edged sword, it penetrates even to dividing soul and spirit, joints and marrow; it judges the thoughts and attitudes of the heart.*

God's word is alive; its power can track us down if we are doing wrong. When the word of God is being preached, we can literally be cut by it. It will convict us of wrongs we are committing. We can run but we can't hide from the truths of God's word.

When I was growing up, there was a man from out of town who was hired to be the Pastor. He had the right talk and the right disposition, but he wasn't a minister of the Gospel. As he preached the word on Sunday mornings, he really put on a great act. He would quote the Scriptures and pound his fist on the pulpit as he was preaching. However, he became convicted by the very word he was preaching. He later confessed to the Board of Deacons that he wasn't called to preach the Gospel. He said that he needed money and he heard that the church was without a Pastor. His wife was convicted also. Around the same time her husband confessed, she confided to one of the Deacons' wives that her husband was a false prophet. Of course, they were immediately dismissed from the church and they moved to another city.

God's word will find us out. We cannot hide from the truth. I realize that there are instances when people continue for years deceiving other people by pretending that they are someone else. Whatever is hidden will eventually come to the light.

In the same manner, the word of God hidden in our hearts can prevent us from sinning against God. Psalm 119:11 (NIV) says: *I have hidden your word in my heart that I might not sin against you.*

We can be faithful with the word of God by keeping it hidden in our heart. You might ask, "Why do we need to hide the word of God in our hearts?" We hide it because Satan has come to steal, kill, and destroy (John 10:10a). He will steal the confidence we have in the word of God if we don't guard it and keep it planted inside. Many people commit sin because Satan talks them out of the truth. We know better; yet we will turn and do the very opposite. On the other hand, when the word of God is thoroughly planted and hidden in our hearts, we will be careful to obey it fully and our lives will be transformed by it.

There was lady who was a new convert to Christianity. Her friends noticed notable changes in her life. One friend asked her, "When did you first notice that your life had changed?"

She replied, "I noticed that my life had changed when I didn't sweep dirt under the rug anymore."

You see, this lady was a maid. Many times when she would clean homes, she would sweep dirt under the rug to save time. When Jesus came into her heart, she automatically discontinued sweeping dirt under the rugs. She now cleans every inch of the homes that have been entrusted into her care. Dishonesty is no longer a part of her new Christian life because she has hidden the word of God in her heart.

God's word tells us in James 1:22 (NIV): *Do not merely listen to the word, and so deceive yourselves. Do what it says.*

I know people who feel self-righteous just because they have attended a church service. They will return home and see people sitting on the front porch and scold them by calling them all kinds of profane names. The neighbors need to see a Christian example in the person who is attending those church services, an example in speech and deed. Let's not deceive ourselves just because we have heard a good sermon. Sure, hearing the word is a good step, but a better step is to be doers of the word.

James 1:23–24 (NIV) says: *Anyone who listens to the word but does not do what it says is like a man who looks at his face in a mirror and, after looking at himself, goes away and immediately forgets what he looks like.*

The word "listen" means to hear attentively with the intent of obeying.

James tells us in God's word that when we hear the word of God, that word is like a mirror. It will point out defects or sin. Once we see the sin in our lives, we must repent, which means to turn from our sin. If we don't repent, we will go away and forget the sin that has been revealed. One of the reasons that we forget what we look like is that we encounter so many people who look a lot worse than we do. Therefore, we think we are all right.

Listening to the word of God is important because faith comes by hearing (Romans 10:17). But to be a hearer of the word and not a doer is a sin before God.

James 1:25 (NIV) says: *But the man who looks intently into the perfect law that gives freedom, and continues to do this, not forgetting what he has heard, but doing it—he will be blessed in what he does.*

The key to being blessed is to obey the word of God without forgetting what we have heard. All of us want to live the blessed life. We will not experience God's best without remembering and doing what His perfect word says.

A Scripture that I have been quoting every day because it pertains to God's blessing for me is found in Psalm 92:12 (NIV). It says: *The righteous will flourish like a palm tree, they will grow like a cedar of Lebanon.*

The above Scripture is my goal, to flourish like a palm tree and to grow like a cedar of Lebanon. The palm tree is abundant and flourishing; the cedar is deeply rooted, strong and tall.

I read a story about a man who was a doer of the word and not a hearer only. This man was a businessman in a well-known company. He decided to go to a revival and when he arrived he saw one of his competitors there as well. The word of God touched his heart to the extent that he went forward and gave his heart to Jesus. His competitor watched him and he said to himself, "I will watch this man for one year to see if there is anything to this Gospel that he just responded to and if I see a change, then I will give my heart to Jesus as well."

This competitor watched the man who had given his heart to Jesus for a full year. He watched this new Christian businessman experience growth and blessings in his business, his social life, family life, and every area of his life. After a year, he gave his heart to Jesus. He told the man whose life he had been watching that his life **convinced** him that there was something to the Christian Gospel and that he had accepted Jesus as a result of watching him for a year.

What a story! Are there people who are convinced by our daily walk? Will people become a Christian after watching us for a year? They will if we are a doer of the word of God and not a hearer only. They will respond if we are faithful with the word of God.

STAY COMMITTED

In order to stay committed, one must realize that there is no plan B. Serving God is an absolute priority. If we enter our relationship with Jesus Christ knowing that we can serve other gods, then that relationship will not thrive. We will not become spiritually mature Christians.

When my husband, Charles, and I were planning our wedding, I asked God to give me a Scripture that would be the key message on all of my correspondences—such as invitations, letters, napkins, etc. The Scripture that God gave to me is found in Song of Solomon 2:16 (KJV). It says: *My beloved is mine, and I am his.*

This Scriptures became ingrained in my head and heart. I visually saw myself belonging to my husband and my husband belonging to me. God has cemented our marriage because of this preconceived commitment to belong to one another. The word "commitment" comes from the Greek verb *paradidomi*, which means to give over or to entrust to one's charge. It means to devote oneself to God (*Vine's Concise Dictionary of Bible Terms*). When we devote ourselves to God, we are set apart for His service. We should not straddle the fence by serving God one day and Satan the next day.

To commit ourselves to God means that we make a promise to bind ourselves to Him and to be obedient to Him. We literally become a living sacrifice as depicted in Romans 12:1 (NIV), which says: *Therefore, I urge you, brothers, in view of God's mercy, to offer your bodies as living sacrifices, holy and pleasing to God—this is your spiritual act of worship.*

When we offer ourselves to God, we present ourselves for acceptance. Just like in the Old Testament days, when an animal was offered as a sacrifice, it had to be accepted by God in order to be an approved sacrifice. If our hearts are truly surrendered to God, then our sacrifice will be accepted by Him. God is looking for those who are truly committed to Him. The Bible says the following in II Chronicles 16:9a (NIV): *For the eyes of the Lord range throughout the earth to strengthen those whose hearts are fully committed to Him.*

I can recall someone asking a minister to demonstrate how they can be totally committed to God. He then took a blank piece of paper and asked them to sign their name at the bottom of the paper. Once they had signed their name at the bottom, he then said for them to allow God to fill in the rest of the page. Trust God to fill in the blank sheet as He wills and as He determines in His heart. After all, God is Omnipotent, Omniscient, and Omnipresent. Shouldn't we trust Him with our whole life?

I will give you three ways that we can stay committed to God. We must first know that we have already been ***commissioned.*** The word "commissioned" means that a task is entrusted to us; to be given an assignment. Jesus has given all Christians the assignment that is specified in the Great Commission that says: *"Go therefore and make disciples of all the nations, baptizing them in the name of the Father and of the Son and of the Holy Spirit, teaching them to observe all things that I have commanded you; and lo, I am with you always, even to the end of the age."* (Matthew 28:19–20[NKJV])

Our assignment or commission is explicit. Let's leave our comfort zone and be about our Father's business. The Apostle Paul did exactly that when he stated the following in II Timothy 1:11–12a (NIV), *"And of this Gospel I was appointed a herald and an apostle and a teacher. That is why I am suffering as I am."*

Paul is in a cold dungeon in prison; he is lonely and will be soon facing death. In his letter to Timothy, his spiritual son, he is explaining what God has commissioned him to do and that we must suffer for the sake of the Gospel. Timothy is young and has a great deal to learn concerning suffering for the cause of Christ. In II Timothy 1:8 (NIV), Paul says: *"So do not be ashamed to testify about our Lord, or ashamed of me his prisoner. But join with me in suffering for the Gospel, by the power of God."* Paul continues to say in II Timothy 2:8–10 (NIV): *"Remember Jesus Christ, raised from the dead, descended from David. This is my Gospel, for which I am suffering even to the point of being chained like a criminal. But God's Word is not chained. Therefore I endure everything for the sake of the elect, that they too may obtain the salvation that is in Christ Jesus, with eternal glory."*

We must suffer for the sake of the Gospel. When we face hardships, we must remember that the Word of God is not limited. We might be bound but the Word of God is not; it has no limits!

A second way we can stay committed is by being ***convinced.*** "Convinced" means to be sure or persuaded; to have faith. One thing I have learned in the ministry is that we must be convinced of what God has called us to do. If not, circumstance can so easily rob us of our confidence. Paul reassures us to his confidence in II Timothy 1:12b (NIV) when he says: *"Yet I am not ashamed, because I know whom I have believed, and am convinced that He is able to guard what I have entrusted to Him for that day."*

God is able to keep us. We must not give up during difficult times. We must not be ashamed of the Gospel. Confide in those that you know are solid and have a solid witness in Christ Jesus. Paul is exhorting Timothy to do the same thing in II Timothy 3:14 (NIV) when he says: *"But as for you, continue in what you have learned and have become convinced of, because you know those from whom you learned it."*

Nothing shall be able to separate us from the love of God. The following Scriptures Romans 8:38–39 (NIV) assure us by saying, *For I am convinced that neither death nor life, neither angels nor demons, neither the present nor the future, nor any powers, neither height nor depth, nor anything else in all creation, will be able to separate us from the love of God that is in Christ Jesus our Lord.*

A third way we can stay committed is by being ***careful.*** "Careful" means to give attention to accuracy or to be watchful. There was a song that I taught my Sunday School class when I taught 2nd and 3rd graders. Some of the lyrics were, "Oh, be careful little hands what you do, for the Father up above is watching down with love; so be careful little hands what you do." The song was very repetitive and continued in that fashion using other parts of the body.

As an adult, the words to that song still resonate in my spirit. We as Christians need to be very careful as we live this life for our Lord.

Ephesians 5:15–16 (NIV) says: *Be very careful, then, how you live—not as unwise but as wise, making the most of every opportunity, because the days are evil.*

II Timothy 2:22–24 (NIV) says: *Flee the evil desires of youth, and pursue righteousness, faith, love and peace, along with those who call on the Lord out of a pure heart. Don't have anything to do with foolish and stupid arguments, because you know they produce quarrels. And the Lord's servant must not quarrel; instead, he must be kind to everyone, able to teach, not resentful.*

The key is to remember that there is no plan "B." It is God's way or no way at all.

CHAPTER EIGHT

THE HABIT OF HOPE

But those who hope in the Lord will renew their strength. They will soar on wings like eagles; they will run and not grow weary, they will walk and not be faint.

Isaiah 40:31 (NIV)

Can you imagine in just twenty-one days you can have the habit of hope? This means that with each new day you can proclaim, "This is the day that the Lord has made; I will rejoice and be glad in it!" These very words will emanate from your spirit. The negative spirit of doubt will cease to exist because you know that God's mercies truly are renewed each day.

What is hope? Hope is the confident expectation of something good. Regardless what the circumstances might be, good can proceed from them. Romans 8:28 (NIV) says: *And we know that in all things God works for the good of those who love Him, who have been called according to His purpose.*

If you are a Christian, you have been called according to God's purpose. You must believe that God wants only good for His children. With that in mind, God wants you to excel during your times of weakness. Satan uses our attitudes of weakness to make us feel defeated; his greatest tool is to make us feel hopeless and discouraged. We must give our weakness to God. If we want to move from weakness to strength, there must be a strength transfer. We must exchange our weakness for God's strength. As a matter of fact, that is the definition of the word "renewed." It means to "exchange" our weakness for God's strength.

Hope always involves waiting. For God to exchange His strength for ours, we must wait on Him and spend time in His presence. Psalm 27:14 NIV says: *Wait for the Lord; be strong and take heart and wait for the Lord.*

One of the most difficult things to do is to wait when our flesh wants to move. When we wait on the Lord, this allows time for our soul to be renewed. I have a power pack that I use when I am traveling to various apartment complexes ministering to children and adults. I plug my CD player into the power pack and it supplies the necessary power that I need in order to play my music. However, when I return home, I have to charge that power pack. The power pack becomes weak in strength because of its use. It is designed to supply limited power; the main power source is electricity. We are similar to that power pack. We as Christians have the power of the Holy Spirit residing inside of us. After hours of witnessing and doing God's will, we need to spend time in God's presence to get re-energized. Once we are strengthened, we can give fully to those in our sphere of influence.

The Apostle Paul had a weakness; he referred to it as a thorn in the flesh. His hope was in Jesus to restore him; so he went to Jesus for deliverance. After pleading with Jesus three times to take his thorn away, Jesus said, *"My grace is sufficient for you, for My power is made perfect in weakness." Therefore I will boast all the more gladly about my weaknesses, so that Christ's power may rest on me. That is why, for Christ's sake, I delight in weaknesses, in insults, in hardships, in persecutions, in difficulties. For when I am weak, then I am strong.* (II Corinthians 12:9–10 NIV)

Jesus is able to restore our strength. We must be willing to surrender to Him to allow the exchange to take place—to exchange our weakness for His strength. God's word tells us in Isaiah 40:31 (NIV): *But those who hope in the Lord will renew their strength. They will soar on wings like eagles. They will run and not grow weary. They will walk and not be faint.*

Hope is the primary ingredient for the renewal of strength. We wait in God's presence waiting and anticipating for Him to refresh us with His power. We must be still and know that God is God!

THE HOPE TO SUCCEED

God wants us to succeed in all that we do. Hope is paramount for any level of success. Proverbs 13:12 (NIV) says: *Hope deferred makes the heart sick.*

This means that when we fail to exercise hope, we will become depressed or sick in our heart. This Scripture helps me to realize the importance of encouraging others. Many times people feel hopeless because of their circumstances. Our job as Christians is to help lift up our brothers and sisters in Christ.

To grow in our habit of hope, we must commit to the Lord whatever we do and our plans will succeed (Proverbs 16:3). Succeed means:

- to turn out well
- to accomplish what is intended
- to be successful (*The World Book Dictionary*)

Jeremiah 29:11 (NIV) says: *"For I know the plans I have for you," declares the Lord, "plans to prosper you and not to harm you, plans to give you hope and a future."*

We must remember that God is not mad at us. He wants us to succeed; His plans are for us to excel and prosper in every area of our lives. There is a story in Numbers 13 whereby a group of spies did not feel that God had the best in mind for them. These spies were negative and they had a critical spirit. We see this account in Numbers 13:27–28 (NIV), which says: *They gave Moses this account: "We went into the land to which you sent us, and it does flow with milk and honey! Here is its fruit. But the people who live there are powerful, and the cities are fortified and very large. We even saw descendants of Anak there."*

These ten spies were focused on the outward. They were not focused on God's ability to deliver them. We must walk by faith and not by sight (II Corinthians 5:7).

Caleb and Joshua were the only two spies who were positive. Even with positive people around us, negative voices can permeate the masses and deter them. Numbers 13:30–31 (NIV) says: *Then Caleb silenced the people before Moses and said, "We should go up and take possession of the land, for we can certainly do it." But the men who had gone up with him said, "We can't attack those people; they are stronger than we are."*

Whenever we are faced with opposition, a great Scripture to quote is Philippians 4:13 (NIV), which says: *I can do all things through Christ who strengthens me.* If God says it, then we can do it!

HOPE THROUGH MY FATHER'S EYES

We must believe what our Heavenly Father says about us. I have learned that God is not mad at me; He is mad about me! He loves me more than I can fathom. I Corinthians

2:9 (NIV) says: *No eye has seen, no ear has heard, no mind has conceived what God has prepared for those who love Him.*

God has so much more in store for us that we have not experienced yet. With each new day, we can expect to experience His goodness because He loves us.

God thinks good thoughts about us all the time. There is no reason any of us should have a low self-image. Psalm 139:17–18 (NIV) says: *How precious are your thoughts about me, O God. They cannot be numbered! I can't even count them; they outnumber the grains of sand! And when I wake up, you are still with me!*

God has promised to be a Father to us. He says in II Corinthians 6:18 (NIV): *"I will be a Father to you, and you will be My sons and daughters," says the Lord Almighty.*

God will do all that a father is expected to do in caring for his children.

The word "father" means:

- Greek word, *pater*
- Originator of life—male parent
- Focus on relationship
- Nourisher, protector, upholder (*Vine's Concise Dictionary of Bible Words*)

Although this definition of a human parent encompasses our Heavenly Father, it is not all inclusive. God is our Abba Father for those who are led by the Spirit of God. Romans 8:14–15 (NIV) says: *Because those who are led by the Spirit of God are sons of God. For you did not receive a spirit that makes you a slave again to fear, but you received the Spirit of sonship. And by Him we cry, "Abba, Father."*

Abba means Father in Aramaic:

- Daddy or Papa
- Sense of warm intimacy and respect

- Shows that God is a loving and approachable Father (*Vine's Concise Dictionary of Bible Words*)

Because of the Holy Spirit, we are sons and daughters of God. As his children, we are heirs. Everything that is in God's Kingdom belongs to us.

Romans 8:17 (NIV) says: *Now if we are children, then we are heirs—heirs of God and co-heirs with Christ, if indeed we share in His sufferings in order that we may also share in His glory.*

As my Heavenly Father, the Lord is my Shepherd and I shall not want (Psalm 23:1). I envision God as a Father who is available to supply all of my needs. He is not limited. Our earthly fathers can mean the best for us, but they are limited in their ability to supply all of our needs. There is no limit with God and nothing is impossible for Him!

OUR BLESSED HOPE

Don't you long for the coming of our Lord and Savior Jesus Christ? That promise is our blessed hope. Blessed hope means the glorious appearing of Jesus Christ. Jesus will return in the same manner that he left. Acts 1:11 (NIV) says: *"Men of Galilee," they said, "Why do you stand here looking into the sky? This same Jesus, who has been taken from you into heaven, will come back in the same way you have seen Him go into heaven."*

If we are born again, which means that Jesus lives inside of us, we can be assured of going to heaven when we die. If we are still alive when Jesus returns, we will be caught up in the cloud and taken up to heaven to live with Him forever.

I Thessalonians 4:16–17 (KJV) says: *For the Lord Himself shall descend from heaven with a shout, with the voice of the archangel, and with the trump of God: and the dead in Christ shall rise first: Then we which are alive and remain shall be caught up together with them in the clouds, to meet the Lord in the air: and so shall we ever be with the Lord.*

Christ in us is the hope of glory (Colossians 1:27). Our ticket to heaven is to have Christ in us. We don't have to walk around in fear. Jesus wants us to watch and wait because no one knows the day or hour when Jesus will return. Matthew 24:44 says that we must be ready, because the Son of Man will come at an hour when we do not expect Him.

Our responsibility as Christians is not only for us to be ready, but our responsibility is to tell others about Jesus so that they too can be ready. The only thing we can take to heaven with us is another soul!

Become a Christian

If you don't know Jesus as your Lord and personal Savior, and you want to become a Christian, just pray the Sinner's Prayer below. Once you have prayed this prayer, you should contact your Pastor or some other spiritual leader and make plans to get baptized. Then you are ready to live a life for Jesus and heaven will be your hope of glory!

Sinner's Prayer

Lord Jesus, I am a sinner. Please forgive me of all my sins, and cleanse me from all unrighteousness. I believe that you died for me on the cross and that you rose again.

Come now, Lord Jesus, and live your life in me. Fill me Lord, with your Holy Spirit. Thank You, Lord, for saving me. In Jesus Name I pray. Amen.

BIBLIOGRAPHY

Holy Bible—New International Version—*The NIV Study Bible*, 10th Anniversary Edition; Copyright 1995 by Zondervan Publishing House; General Editor—Kenneth Barker; Associate Editors—Donald Burdick, John Stek, Walter Wessel, Ronald Youngblood

The Holy Bible containing the Old and New Testaments; New King James Version (NKJV); Giant Print Center-Column Reference Edition; Thomas Nelson Bibles; Copyright 1994

The Holy Bible, TBN Parallel Bible; King James Version (KJV) and New Living Translation (NLT); Tyndale House Publishers, Inc., Copyright 2005

Vine's Concise Dictionary of Bible Words, author W.E. Vine; Thomas Nelson Publishers, Nashville; copyright 1999

Webster's New Compact Dictionary for School and Office—Revised Edition. Walter C. Kidney, Editor; Thomas Nelson Publishers, copyright 1991

The World Book Dictionary, Clarence L. Barnhart, Editor in Chief; Volume One (A–K); Field Enterprises Educational Corporation; copyright 1974

The World Book Dictionary, Clarence L. Barnhart, Editor in Chief; Volume Two (L–Z); Field Enterprises Educational Corporation; copyright 1974

MEET THE AUTHOR

Pastor Earnestine Blakley is a native of Steele, Missouri—located in the Missouri Boot Hill. She currently resides in St. Joseph, Missouri, with her husband, Charles; they have two adult sons—Charles Jr. and Andrew.

Pastor Blakley is the Pastor and Founder of Hope Fellowship Church in St. Joseph, Missouri. She—along with the help and support of her husband, Charles—founded this nondenominational ministry on June 4, 2009. The mission is to proclaim the Gospel of Jesus Christ so that others may know Him and make Him known through Evangelism, Worship, and Discipleship.

Pastor Blakley is also the founder and President of H.O.P.E. Outreach Ministries, Inc., founded on June 13, 1994. (H.O.P.E. is an acronym for Helping Other People Excel.) The mission of this outreach ministry is to help the hurting and the needy find hope and spiritual nourishment through God's Word. Pastor Blakley and numerous volunteers read storybooks to children at apartment complexes during the summer months. During the school year, she arranges for students from local schools to visit the elderly in nursing homes so they can interact through games and conversation. Some of the objectives are to promote literacy, build relationships, foster volunteerism, and to break down generational, socioeconomic, cultural, and denominational barriers.

Pastor Blakley taught in the St. Joseph School District for fourteen years. During the 1991–92 school year, she was named St. Joseph Teacher of the Year and the Missouri State Teacher of the Year. She has served on the National Education Panel for Energizer Battery, the State Committee for America 2000, the State Commission on Performance, and the National Writing Team for the Environmental Protection Agency. On April 20, 2011, she received the Roy Blunt Literacy Citation; on April 18, 2012, she received the Missouri Humanities Exemplary Community Achievement Award for Youth Literacy from the Missouri Humanities Council in Jefferson City, Missouri.

During her teaching career, she was named "Woman of Distinction" for the Midland Empire Girl Scout Council; she has been listed in the *World's Who's Who of Women*, and the *Who's Who in American Education*; she was nominated for the Walt Disney American Teacher Awards, and was a National Finalist for Project Self-Esteem.

Currently, Pastor Blakley has a weekly ministry on KQ2 TV every Sunday morning at 9:00 a.m. and a weekly radio ministry on KSJI Radio 91.1 FM every Sunday morning at 9:30 a.m. In foreign ministry, Pastor Blakley has preached and ministered in Guatemala, Venezuela, and the Bahamas.

Pastor Earnestine Blakley has a Bachelor of Science Degree in Elementary Education from Lincoln University in Jefferson City, Missouri; a Master of Science Degree in Education from Northwest Missouri State University in Maryville, Missouri; an Honorary Doctorate of Humane Letters Degree from Maryville University in St. Louis, Missouri; Credentialing as an Ordained Minister from Global University of the Assemblies of God in Springfield, Missouri; and a Writing Diploma from the Institute of Children's Literature in Redding Ridge, Connecticut.

CPSIA information can be obtained
at www.ICGtesting.com
Printed in the USA
FFHW02n1353050918
48141249-51861FF

9 781629 011936